Lester Frank Ward

Haeckel's genesis of man, or history of the development of the

human race

being a review of his

Lester Frank Ward

Haeckel's genesis of man, or history of the development of the human race
being a review of his

ISBN/EAN: 9783742815699

Manufactured in Europe, USA, Canada, Australia, Japa

Cover: Foto ©Thomas Meinert / pixelio.de

Manufactured and distributed by brebook publishing software
(www.brebook.com)

Lester Frank Ward

Haeckel's genesis of man, or history of the development of the human race

PREFACE.

THE three papers constituting this little *brochure* were originally contributed to the PENN MONTHLY, and appeared in the April, May, and July numbers of that magazine for 1877.

As the work which it was their more especial object to review has not yet been placed before the non-German reading public, no apology is offered for their reproduction in separate form.

In view, however, of the popular interest which the views of Prof. Haeckel have since called forth, and which seems to be still increasing, it was thought an opportune moment for laying before the general public this condensed exposition of the thought and labors of the great naturalist and philosopher.

It may further interest the reader to learn that Prof. Haeckel has acknowledged, in a private communication to the author, the substantial correctness with which these papers represent his position.

L. F. W.

Washington, March, 1879.

HAECKEL'S GENESIS OF MAN, OR HISTORY OF THE DEVELOPMENT OF THE HUMAN RACE.[1]

I.

IT is no derogation from the epoch-making labors of Charles Darwin to admit that the arguments he has presented in support of his celebrated theory constitute, as it were, but the half of the vast array which the present state of biological science is capable of marshalling in its defence.

The sources from which the evidences of descent and natural selection must be derived, may be divided into two general classes: *First*, Paleontology, Comparative Anatomy and Osteology, and Geographical Distribution (*Chorology*), *i. e.*, a comparison of the adult forms of animals both living and fossil (*Phylogeny*); and *Second*, the study of embryonic changes and post-natal metamorphoses, or a comparison of undeveloped animal forms (*Ontogeny*). Of these two classes it may be said that the first have been furnished by Darwin, the second by Haeckel. Not that Darwin, either in his *Origin of Species* or in his *Descent of Man*, has wholly ignored the bearing of embryological considerations upon his theory. In the former work he has devoted seventeen pages of one of his concluding chapters to "Development and Embryology;" the greater part of which, however, is occupied in pointing out the importance of the various kinds of metamorphosis, chiefly as it is observed in insects, amphibians, etc., after birth; only incidentally referring to those more obscure metamorphoses which take place within the egg or the uterus.

He does allude, however, more directly to Von Baer's law, but without designating it as such; and contents himself with quoting the passage, cited also by Haeckel in the preface to the third edition of his *History of Creation* (1870), in which the great Russian embryologist remarks upon the striking similarity of many em-

---

[1] Anthropogenie, oder Entwickelungsgeschichte des Menschen, von Ernst Haeckel, Professor an der Universität Jena. Leipsic, 1874.

bryos, so much so that he was quite unable to say to what animals two specimens which he had preserved in alcohol but had neglected to label, really belonged. Still less attention has Darwin paid to this source of argument in his *Descent of Man*. A few lines quoted from Von Baer and from Huxley, on page 14 of Vol. 1, a figure of the embryo of a human being and one of a dog, from Ecker, on page 15, with brief comments, disposes of this branch of his great argument. Almost as much had been said by the author of the *Vestiges of Creation*, in 1842.[2] It is safe, therefore, to assume that at the time of the appearance of the *Origin of Species* (1859), Darwin had no conception of the real part that the arguments from embryology were destined to play in establishing his doctrine of the development of organic forms. And although in subsequent editions he was able to notice the *Generelle Morphologie*, it is still improbable that even then he had any adequate idea of the powerful ally he was to have in Germany, as the *Natürliche Schöpfungsgeschichte*, and not less the work under review, have proved the professor of Jena to be. It is of the former of these works that Darwin says that if it had appeared before the *Descent of Man* had been written, he would probably never have completed the latter.

Professor Haeckel is no mere disciple of Darwin, profound as is his admiration of him, and unreserved as is his expression of that admiration. His own countrymen have accused him of being "more Darwinistic than Darwin himself," but it is clear that a large part of this difference is in kind rather than in degree, and that he has infused into the developmental philosophy a true Haeckelian element. It is true that he drew the logical conclusion from the premises furnished by the *Origin of Species* five years before the announcement of its recognition by Darwin himself in his *Descent of Man*. This conclusion he boldly and forcibly enunciated in the introduction to his *Generelle Morphologie*, published in 1866, and reiterated with still greater emphasis in his *Natürliche Schöpfungsgeschichte*, in 1868. Between this period and that of the appearance of the *Descent of Man*, Haeckel was exposed to the bitterest attacks, not only from the adherents of the Church and the opponents of Darwin generally, but from those adherents of Darwinism in Germany—and they were many—whose conception

2 New York, 1845, p. 150.

of it was limited to the body of principles contained in the *Origin of Species*. As in that work all reference to the position of the human race in the animal kingdom was carefully excluded, thus ingeniously avoiding the shock of prejudice which any such connection would have occasioned, the simplicity, the *naïveté*, and, at the same time, the force of reasoning displayed in it, not only won the immediate assent of all fully emancipated minds, but took a strong hold upon great numbers of liberally educated persons whose independent reflections had not yet carried them wholly out from under the influence of theological conceptions. Among these were many thoroughly scientific men and naturalists, specialists in the various departments of science, whose analytical labors had not left them time for a synthesis of the facts even within their own special branch of research. These accepted the conclusions drawn in the *Origin of Species* without perceiving that other and important ones might and must follow from the same premises. And because Haeckel drew these logical and necessary conclusions, these persons attacked him from all sides, and heaped upon him every form of accusation. Besides the charge above referred to of out-Darwining Darwin, and of going further than Darwin himself would ever sanction, there was added the stronger one that Haeckel knew nothing about true Darwinism. The appearance in 1871 of Darwin's *Descent of Man* placed these anti-Haeckel Darwinians in a most embarrassing situation, silencing many, converting numbers, and driving not a few into the theological camp. But Haeckel emerged majestically from the battle, unscathed and undaunted. To charges of " radicalism " he had simply replied : " Radical thinking is consistent thinking, which allows itself to be checked by no barriers of tradition or of enforced dogma." To the confused outcry of the theological school and of the anti-Darwinians in general, he did not deem it worth his while to reply. A satirical remark upon this class, however, is worth reproducing and might be ranked alongside of Darwin's cutting sarcasm, wherein he says that he who scorns to be descended from a beast will generally reveal his descent in the act of sneering, whereby he will expose his canine teeth. " It is an interesting and instructive circumstance," says Haeckel, " that just those persons are most shocked and indignant at the discovery of the natural development of the human race from the apes, who, in their intellectual development and cerebral differentiation, are obviously least removed from our common tertiary ancestors."

Both in his *History of Creation* and in his *Anthropogeny*, Haeckel has done a service to the cause of evolution by reviewing, in a fair and disinterested manner, the history of the origin and progress of those ideas which have culminated in the Darwinian theory. Let us glance for a moment at this history.

Passing over the names of Wolff, Baer, Kant, Schleiden, Oken, and Humboldt, in Germany, of Buffon and Geoffrey St. Hilaire, in France, and of Dean Herbert, Professor Grant, Patrick Matthew, Freke, and Herbert Spencer (*Essays, 1852*), in England, all of whom had given more or less definite expression to these progressive ideas prior to the appearance of the *Origin of Species*, it may be remarked that the great conception of the natural relationship (filiation) of all organic forms and their descent or development from common ancestors that have existed in more or less remote periods of the past, had a threefold independent origin in the minds of three men who were contemporary at the close of the last and the beginning of the present century, in each of the three great nations that now lead the intellectual world. These men were Erasmus Darwin, grandfather of the illustrious Charles, in England, Wolfgang Goethe, the great poet and philosopher, in Germany, and Jean Lamarck, in France. Wholly unacquainted with each other and with each other's works, these three men, almost at the same time, gave utterance to substantially the same fundamental ideas, and elaborated in more or less extended and systematic form the essential ground-principles which now underlie the edifice of all progressive biological science.

In his work entitled *Zoönomia*, published in 1794, Erasmus Darwin lays great weight upon the transformation of species of animals and plants through their own activities of life and through forced habituation to changed conditions of existence. It is a current remark, as applied to Charles Darwin, that he furnishes in himself one of the finest illustrations of " development," and thus of the truth of his own theory, that can be cited. Far more pointed, however, is the pleasantry of Haeckel, when, referring to the grandfather of Charles as entertaining the germs of his grandson's philosophy, and noting the striking circumstance that his father, though a respectable physician, exhibited no signs of having inherited these intellectual characteristics, he cites the case as a good example of "atavism," and remarks that "Erasmus Darwin transmitted, according to the law of latent inheritance, definite molecular motions in the ganglion cells of his cerebrum to his grandson Charles without their manifesting themselves in his son Robert."

The importance of Erasmus Darwin's views, however, mixed as they were with some vagaries and unbalanced speculations, was slight as compared with that which we must ascribe to those of Goethe. In his various essays and writings on "Natural Science" in general (1780), on Comparative Anatomy and Osteology (1786), on the Metamorphoses of Plants (1790), and in later works, he has wrought out a philosophy of organic life, which, when carefully analyzed and translated into the terminology now adopted, is found to contain, in their most general and fundamental form, the essential principles of the Darwinian theory of development. A few passages will illustrate this. In 1706 he wrote: "All the more perfect organic natures, under which we see fishes, amphibians, birds, mammals, and, at the head of these last, man, are formed according to one original type (*Urbild*), which in its durable parts only deviates more or less, and is still daily being improved and transformed through propagation." It is from this and other passages in which Goethe establishes his doctrine of an original type or image, which varies only slightly and in detail and not in plan, that the modern adherents of the theory of fixed types seem to have derived their chief arguments. Cuvier must have been conversant with Goethe's scientific writings, and he may have drawn largely upon them in founding his celebrated system of classification. But like some other great works that have become authority, those of Goethe are found, in some things, to admit of two interpretations, and to supply texts looking more than one way. The above passage, taken in connection with others, is now seen still more clearly to give countenance to what is now the powerful rival of the doctrine of types : viz., the doctrine of descent. In another place he says : "An internal original community (*Gemeinschaft*) lies at the bottom of all organization ; difference of form, on the contrary, arises from the necessary relations to the external world, and we may, therefore, with right assume an original, simultaneous variation and an incessantly progressive transformation, in order to comprehend the at once constant and deviating phenomena."

To further explain this paradox he assumes two independent forces or impulses, working harmoniously together in nature, an internal formative impulse (*innerer Bildungstrieb*), and an external formative impulse (*äusserer Bildungstrieb*). The former of these he also, in different passages, designates as the specific force (*Specifica-tionstrieb*) and as the centripetal force ; the latter, on the other hand, he calls the modifying force or impulse of variation (*Variationstrieb*, and the centrifugal force. He also uses the term metamorphosis in a general (phylogenetic) sense as applied to the changes that take place in species and genera rather than in individuals. The following passage contains the kernel of this entire portion of his philosophy: " The idea of metamorphosis is like that of the *vis centrifuga*, and would lose itself in infinity were there not a check offered to it ; this check is the specific force (*Specificationstrieb*), the stubborn power of permanency (*zähe Beharrlichkeitsvermögen*) of whatever has once become a reality, a *vis centripeta*, which in its deepest foundations can possess no externality."

If, now, we translate Goethe's internal formative impulse, specific force, or centripetal force, by the modern term *heredity*, as we undoubtedly may, and his external formative impulse, modifying force, or centrifugal force, by the modern term *adaptation*, as we may still more clearly do, we shall have, in Goethe's philosophy of life, neither more nor less than the essential elements of the modern doctrine of descent.

Of course, nothing is here found but the general principles ; the mode and the examples could not have been furnished in Germany when Goethe wrote.

Haeckel, however, is abundantly justified in pointing to Germany's greatest genius as having long ago given utterance to the most radical of his own doctrines and that for which he has received the severest animadversions, when, in the passage first quoted, he places man at the head of the mammalian class. And yet, who had thought of assailing Goethe with the charge of deriving man from the apes !

With almost equal justice does Haeckel claim that, in the following and other passages, Goethe has not only declared the genealogical relationship of the vegetable to the animal kingdom, but has furnished the nucleus of the unitary or monophyletic theory of descent. " When we consider plants and animals in their most imperfect condition they are scarcely to be distinguished. This much, however, we may say, that those creatures that now and then ap-appear, having relationships with plants and with animals difficult to separate, perfect themselves in two opposite directions, so that the plant at last glorifies itself in the tree, durable and fixed, the animal, in man, with the highest degree of mobility and freedom."

The ambiguity of Goethe's language is due to the profundity and high generality of his ideas, coupled with a certain poetic vagueness so indispensable to his genius. In the former quality, though not at all in the latter, one is reminded of that profound and comprehensive analysis which, with all the materials of that later date (1866), and with the power of logic characteristic of England's foremost philosopher, Herbert Spencer, in his *Biology*, (vol. I, ch. xi., and xii.), has made of these same principles; a treatise, I may add, which Haeckel has indeed recognized,[3] but upon which he could scarcely have failed to place more emphasis if he had been thoroughly acquainted with it.

Quite different in method and character from Goethe's contribution to the theory of transmutation and descent was that of La-marck. Whatever his philosophy may have lacked in profundity, it was not open to the charge of ambiguity. All its shortcomings were amply compensated for by the wealth of illustration and the multiplicity of facts drawn directly from nature, which, as a life-long naturalist, he was able to bring to its support. In this respect (and this is after all the chief consideration), the now celebrated, though long neglected, *Philosophie Zoologique* is alone, of all the works that had preceded it or were contemporary with it, worthy of a serious comparison with the *Origin of Species* or the *Descent of Man*. And it is certainly a remarkable coincidence and may have for some readers, if no other, at least a mnemonic value, that the *Philosophie Zoologique* and the *Origin of Species* were separated by the space of just half a century, the former appearing in 1809, the latter in 1859. The interest of this circumstance is still further heightened by the fact that Charles Darwin was born in the year 1809, the same in which the great precursor of his own works like-wise issued into the world; as if its subtle influence had wafted across the channel and breathed its mysterious *afflatus* into the nostrils of the new-born herald of its principles!

[3] Schöpfungsgeschichte, 5 Aufl. pp. 106, 657.

The dim intimations and scattered glimpses of Goethe and of Dr. Darwin were insignificant in comparison with the lucid illustrations and systematic arguments of the great French naturalist. After so many years of assiduous study Lamarck, as it were, but copied his conclusions from the pages of nature where facts stood forth like letters in a book. Yet none the less credit to his intellect, for was not this same book sealed to his great contemporary, Cuvier, who knew its alphabet equally well? And is it not sealed to many to-day? The truth is that for the first time the causal and essentially rational type of mind had been joined in the same individual with those other qualities which impel to the patient investigation of facts and details; rare combination, so successfully repeated in the intellectual constitutions of Charles Darwin and Ernst Haeckel.

When we compare, from our disinterested standpoint in America, the great *chef d' œuvre* of Jean Lamarck, its systematic execution, its definite, avowed purpose, and its vast array of proofs from the only legitimate source of argument, with the various writings of Goethe containing his views on this subject, arranged with no systematic order, having no well defined purpose, evincing no clear conception of nature's means or methods, and manifesting a comparatively scanty acquaintance with particular cases by which the laws under discussion are to be illustrated, we cannot fail to perceive, in the circumstance of Haeckel's placing his own countryman before the son of a rival nation, in his estimate of the relative labors of the two pioneers of evolution, a trace of that almost inevitable national bias which lurks in regions of the brain inaccessible to the invasion even of exact science. The essential incongruity between the first and last parts of the following passage will be apparent to all. "At the head of the French natural philosophy stands Jean Lamarck, who, in the history of the doctrine of descent, next to Darwin *and Goethe*, occupies the first place. To him will remain the immortal glory of having for the first time brought forward the theory of descent as an independent scientific theory and established it as the natural philosophical foundation of all biology." He certainly ascribes to Goethe no such "immortal glory" as this.

There is but one distinct element in Darwinism that is not also found in Lamarckism. This is the important recognition of the law of competition among living organisms as a factor in development; that principle which Darwin so forcibly expresses by the phrase "struggle for existence." Lamarck does indeed recognize this "struggle" and the influence it exerts in preventing the unchecked multiplication of any one species from rendering the globe uninhabitable to others. But he seems to regard this as a wise precaution and calculated "to preserve all in the established order." In other words, he recognizes it as a *statical* but not as a *dynamical* law. He fails to perceive its influence in transforming species.

It is the full appreciation of this element that constitutes the real strength of Darwinism; it is the key-stone of the arch of the descent theory, for the discovery and successful illustration of which too great praise cannot be awarded to the English naturalist. But every other important principle embraced in his *Origin of Species* was also contained in more or less definite form in the *Philosophie Zoologique.*

The failure of Lamarck's views to gain the ascendancy so rapidly attained by those of Darwin, was due to a variety of causes. First among these was the general fact that the state of science and public opinion had not, at his time, sufficiently advanced for the general reception of that class of ideas; and any estimate of Lamarck's works which leaves out their silent, leavening influence upon certain classes directly, and thence indirectly upon society at large, is too hastily made and fails to do them justice. Next in importance, in preventing the early spread of Lamarckism, comes the unfortunate omission, above alluded to, to grasp the great law of biological competion in its dynamic form. As a third influence may be ranked the somewhat direct and undiplomatic method of Lamarck, which never consulted the policy of what he wished to say or courted the approval of high authorities. Every truth in his possession was put forward in the most direct and naked manner, regardless of the shock it might produce upon a world still groping in the murky atmosphere of teleology. Still a fourth element of weakness in the Lamarckian philosophy was the inadequate emphasis which he laid upon the most important of all his principles, that of heredity, and the correspondingly undue importance ascribed to habit, to use and disuse, as a direct agent in the modification of organs. The real failure here was to grasp the true connection and cöoperation of these two principles. In short he seemed but dimly to perceive the manner in which the inheritance of slight variations, however produced, and their transmission to successive generations, brings about, in the course of time, the transformation of some, and the extinction of other species. It is the clear conception and forcible presentation of this principle and its happy combination with that of the perpetual competition going on in nature, that gives to Darwin's exposition that air of extreme probability and that power of universal conviction so characteristic of his works. The importance of this distinction between the methods of the two naturalists in expressing this conception may justify me in borrowing a few very appropriate terms from the *Biology* of Herbert Spencer for its better illustration. We may then say that while Lamarck seemed clearly to comprehend the influence of the *environment (milieu)* upon the *organism*, and to attribute the results to this as the one great and sufficient cause, he failed on the one hand to take in the full scope of the environment, and on the other to conceive of all the susceptibilities of the organism.   In his conception of the former he inadequately, if at all, appreciated the organic element, the influence of one organism upon another objectively considered as a modifying force. In his notion of the organism and its susceptibilities he laid too great stress upon the principle of "*direct equilibration*," and comparatively little upon the far more important one of "*indirect equilibration.*" To the readers of the *Philosophic Zoologique* it seemed a crude, to many a ridiculous, explanation of the length of the fore-limbs and neck of the giraffe, that they had become elongated by perpetual attempts to reach the branches of trees that lay beyond the reach of other animals ; and while he admits that this could not have been accomplished by the efforts of any single individual, and ascribes it to a series of cumulative efforts through many generations, thus clearly recognizing and expressly affirming the influence of heredity, he yet fails to show the way in which this influence must have been exerted, its *modus operandi*.   He does not say, for example, that the great elongation referred to was initiated in some remote ancestor by some slight variation in this direction, either accidental or perhaps due to the animal's efforts ; that this variation, proving advantageous and being transmitted to a numerous progeny, rendered their chances of survival in critical periods greater than those of such as possessed no such peculiarity ; that this power of survival, due to this inheritable peculiarity, became thus a constant force which, through the interbreeding of those possessing it, tended to increase this variation, until in the course of generations it resulted in differentiating the giraffe in the special attributes of length of cervical vertebræ and of anterior limbs, and in giving it its present anomalous position among antelopes. Instead of this, Lamarck says: "With reference to habits it is curious to observe their results in the peculiar form and figure of the giraffe (*camelo-pardalis*). It is known that this animal, the tallest of the mammals, inhabits the interior of Africa, and that it lives in places where the earth, almost always arid and without herbage, compels it to browse upon the leaves of trees and to be continually exerting itself to reach them. From this habit, long maintained in all the individuals of its race, it *has resulted* that its fore-limbs have become longer than its hind ones, and that its neck has become so much elongated that the giraffe, without rearing upon its hind feet elevates its head and reaches to the height of six mètres, (nearly twenty feet)."[4] It will be observed how in this reasoning (and it is so throughout), Lamarck passes from the observed fact directly to the original cause, leaving out the intermediate steps which it is necessary to supply in order to conceive of the manner in which the results are produced. Now, it is precisely this part of the argument that mankind in general require before they are willing to give in their adhesion to a theory. They say: "it all looks plausible enough, but you fail to show us *how* it actually takes place." As in his illustrations, so in his general "laws," Lamarck fails to grasp the principle of Natural Selection. His first great law is expressed in these words: "In every animal which has not passed the limit of its developments, the frequent and sustained use of any organ little by little strengthens, develops, and enlarges this organ, and gives it a power proportionate to the duration of this exercise; while the constant failure to use such organ insensibly enfeebles and deteriorates it, and progressively diminishes its capacities, causing it finally to disappear."[5] His second law is as follows: "All that nature has caused individuals to acquire or lose through the influence of the circumstances to which their race has been long exposed, and consequently through the influence of the

[4] Phil. Zoo., Tome I, p. 254. Paris, 1873.
[5] Loc. cit., p. 235.

predominant exercise of any organ, or through that of a constant
failure to exercise any part, it preserves through inheritance (*géné-
ration*) in the new individuals that proceed from them, provided
the changes acquired be common to both sexes, or to those which
have produced these new individuals."[6]

Whatever may be lacking in these two laws, there is certainly
contained in them a clear expression of the two prime factors of
the theory of descent : viz., heredity and variation ; or, as Darwin
frequently expresses it, " descent with modification." The elements
of availability alone are wanting ; those working principles by
which the theory was to be erected into a perfect system and its
machinery set into running order.

A grand stride had been made, the doctrine of fixity of species
had received a fatal thrust, the special creation hypothesis was un-
dermined, teleology thenceforth was in organic nature doomed.

A fifth and last element of weakness in the Lamarckian philosophy may be enumerated, one which Haeckel justly sets down to
the greater credit of the illustrious author as indicating how far he
had outstripped the intellectual progress of his age, so that it was
practically impossible that his views should have been accepted in
his own day. This consisted in the acceptance and express enun-
ciation of two doctrines which are still to-day deeply involved in
controversy, even among the most advanced scientific men of our
times ; that of *spontaneous generation* and that of the *simian ancestry of the human race*, embracing in the latter the extreme theory
of the development of the mind *pari passu* with that of the nervous
system and the brain, and carrying it out to the logical consequence
of denying the freedom of the will, in the current sense of the
phrase. These were clearly, in Lamarck's day, shocking and atro-
cious doctrines, and it is doubtless to these chiefly that is to be
attributed the neglect of his great contemporary, Cuvier, to give
the *Philosophie Zoologique* as much as a passing notice in his report
on the progress of natural science ; as well as the rebuke of his
philosophical views which he saw fit to introduce into his " éloge " (?)
of the great scientific labors of Lamarck. He little dreamed that
when these utterances should have been forgotten, and the works
of Cuvier consigned to the musty shelves of antiquarian libraries,
the humble effort which he had first disdained to notice and after-

[6] Loc. cit.

wards noticed with a reproach, would emerge from its long obscurity, and, in new and modern dress, find its way to thousands of book ·tables, as the classic foundation of a great progressive philosophy.

With regard to Lamarck's views on the subject of spontaneous generation, it is due to him to say that he did not espouse any of the crude conceptions which had been maintained on the authority of Aristotle among the scholastic metaphysicians. He repeatedly asserts that it is only the most imperfectly organized beings that could be directly produced by the forces of inorganic nature, and while he could have had but a faint idea of the extreme imperfection of these lowliest creatures, still as only the *least* perfectly organized could, according to him, become the products of spontaneous generation, his careful language on this point completely exempts him from the charge of entertaining gross notions about the origin of life. Haeckel, with his intimate acquaintance with the lowest known forms of organic existence, his *moncra*, does not hesitate to declare the necessity of a transition, at some period, from the inorganic to the organic condition; nay, more, he believes that these *moncra* are directly evolved, by the mechanical agencies of nature, out of inorganic carbon compounds, and that protoplasm, of which alone these creatures consist, is the initial stage of organic life. With Lamarck, as with Haeckel, it is the logical necessity, rather than any empirical discovery, that renders this doctrine indispensable as a starting point and first link in the chain of organic development. As the latter justly remarks, unless we do this the natural explanation is given up, and there remains no alternative but to fall back upon the supernatural. Herbert Spencer, too, independently of his theory of physiological units, has felt the force of this *a priori* argument, and has ranged himself on the side of complete consistency. Neither need the teleologists exult at the apparent overthrow, just now so imminent, of the results of Bastian's experiments. From such a result we shall only the better learn *how* nature works, and no adherent of the doctrine of *archigonia* will the less maintain that life must have had a beginning upon the planet. Lamarck leans to the assumption of a perpetual series of such beginnings which are still going on in the present as in the past, a constant play of the originating force. Haeckel admits as much for protoplasm and for his *moncra ;* beyond this he says it does not concern the theory of descent to go. Darwin, with his characteristic diplomacy, never lifts the dark curtain that hangs between the organic and the inorganic world.

Professor Haeckel is not only an original investigator, but also an original thinker. Primarily a specialist and investigator of the minute histology of living organisms, there is combined in his mental constitution, along with this indispensable talent, a large development of causality which renders it impossible for him to stop with the mere elaboration of details and the simple accumulation of facts. To him every fact is one of the terms of a proposition, and every collection of related facts becomes an argument, while the sum total of his knowledge of those minute creatures which he has made a life study constitutes in his mind a philosophy. He is at once an investigator and a philosopher. To the former quality, his numerous monographs of the lower invertebrates sufficiently testify. His monograph of the *Radiolaria* (with an atlas of thirty-five copper plates), of the *Geryonidae*, of the *Siphonopora*, but especially of the calcareous sponges, belong to the minutest and most exhaustive histological researches of modern zoology. In all these, but particularly in the last named, the author has constantly before him a theorem to demonstrate. He expressly avows that his investigations into the calcareous sponges were undertaken with a view to an analytical solution of the problem of the origin of species. He seems not to have feared thus to invite the charge of having resolved, in this investigation, to verify the argument of Darwin, the perusal of whose great work had induced him to undertake it. Nor does he fail to prove all he hoped to do. On the contrary, he claims to have overwhelmingly established all the principal claims of his English contemporary. The objection had been raised that the Darwinian theory did not rest upon a sufficient body of observed facts ; that it was a mere plausible synthesis from a too meagre analysis. Haeckel holds up his two volumes, containing the results of his five years of indefatigable labor on these lower organisms, and his atlas with its sixty carefully drawn plates, all elaborated from the most abundant materials from all parts of the world, and challenges the scrutiny of his scientific opponents. The doctrine of the fixity and invariability of species, already reeling under the blows of Lamarck and Darwin, he claims, is therein completely demolished. He proves that in this group of animals the number of genera and species depends altogether upon the meaning which each naturalist may happen to attach to these terms. He may class them all under one genus with three species, or under three genera with twenty-one species, or under twenty-one genera with 111 species, or under thirty-nine genera with 289 species, or even under 113 genera with 591 species, according as his conception of genera and species be wide or narrow. In fact, the 591 different forms may be so arranged in a genealogical tree that the ancestry of the entire group can be traced back to one common form from which all the rest must have descended, undergoing the modifications induced by the varying conditions of their existence. This common ancestor Haeckel believes to be the *Olynthus*.

Thus, the long respected and miraculously created *bona species* is histologically demonstrated a myth.

Rising from the special towards the general, the *Generelle Morphologie* may be next named. It was the first systematic attempt to establish the theory of development from the organized facts of comparative anatomy. But the most popular, in its subject matter and style, of the works of Professor Hackel is his *Natürliche Schöpfungsgeschichte*, consisting of a course of lectures upon the questions in general opened by the *Origin of Species*, but containing the advanced views of the author, already referred to. This work is, therefore, of the highest interest to the general public, and cannot be too strongly recommended. It is divided into five parts designated by the author with the following titles, respectively, each of which sufficiently characterizes its contents: 1, Historical Part; 2, Darwinistic Part; 3, Cosmogenetic Part; 4, Phylogenetic Part; and 5, Anthropogenetic Part.

His *Anthropogeny* or *History of the Development of Man*, to which we will now confine our attention more closely, is simply an enlargement and expansion of the last part of the *History of Creation*. The greatness of the theme required this, and no one who carefully follows the author through this work will complain that justice has not been done the subject. As may well be imagined this work covers the most interesting field of investigation and introduces the reader into the most mysterious penetralia of nature. The charm of its diction, the fullness of its illustrations, and above all the perpetual wonderland through which it leads, entitle it to take rank at once among the most instructive and the most fascinating works to which modern science has ever yet given birth.

"The proper study of mankind is man." And yet how tame
appear the most mysterious facts of human anatomy and physi-
ology, as taught to the mass of mankind, compared with the astonishing revelations of comparative embryology and comparative
anatomy!

As already remarked, Haeckel is a philosopher as well as an investigator. No German philosopher can be without his terminology.
Haeckel has his, and it remains to the future to decide whether the
ends of science are to be furthered by its introduction. It is at
least certain that to understand Haeckel one must understand his
terminology. Being much of it of Greek derivation, it undergoes
little change by transfer to the English language. In so far, however, as it is German, this difficulty is great, often, indeed, quite
insuperable. Everybody admits the inadequacy of some parts of
Darwin's terminology. The best English expounders of his theory
have found themselves compelled to adopt other terms to convey
his ideas with the requisite clearness and force. I have already
referred to important improvements introduced by Herbert Spencer before it was possible for him properly to arrange the new
biological laws under his universal system of cosmical principles.
That author has also, in addition to those before referred to, pro-
posed an excellent synonym for Darwin's most important term,
"Natural Selection." This he calls "Survival of the fittest,"
which, while it can never of course supersede the former, must be
admitted by all to bring to the mind far more directly, the idea
which it is desired to convey.

Haeckel has felt the need of some adequate terms to characterize
the two great classes or types of mind, which not only now, but in
all ages, have existed in a state of opposition or rivalry in the
world. No matter what questions might arise for solution bearing
upon the knowledge or progress of the race, there has always existed this sharply defined opposition growing out of these two
constutionally opposite mental types. Various popular appella-
tions have been employed from time to time, differing in different
countries and for different forms of agitation. None of these, however, have struck at the true psychological root of the phenomenon,
and the world has been long waiting for a thorough analysis of this
subject and the suggestion of a scientific terminology, based upon
this ground-law of the constitutional polarity of the human intellect.

That Haeckel has fully supplied this want I would not venture to affirm, but that he has made an important contribution towards such a consummation cannot be questioned. " If," says he, " you place all the forms of cosmological conception of the various peoples and times into comparative juxtaposition, you can finally bring them all into two squarely opposing groups : a *causal* or *mechanical*, and a *teleological* or *vitalistic* group."

The first of these groups, by requiring every phenomenon to be conceived as the mechanical effect of an antecedent true cause (*causa efficiens*), necessarily erects a cosmogony that is bound together throughout by an unbroken chain of mechanically dependent phenomena. Such a universe is a unit, and throughout its domain there can pervade but one universal law. This all-pervading homogeneous law is the *monistic* principle or force, while the whole theory which thus conceives of the universe is termed by Haeckel, indifferently, the *monistic*, and the *mechanical* theory of the universe. Only those minds that are imbued with this conception as a fundamental quality of their cerebral constitution are capable of appreciating, or of subscribing to the Darwinian and Lamarckian philosophy, which is simply the monistic principle applied to biology. This class has formed in all ages and countries the progressive and reformatory element of mankind.

The teleological or vitalistic group, on the other hand, conceive of all phenomena as produced by a power either outside of nature and acting upon it, or consisting of Nature regarded as a conscious intelligence, and which, in either case, directs everything for an ordained purpose or end (*causa finalis*). This recognition of a cause independent of phenomena renders the operations of nature *dual*, and is designated by Haeckel as the *dualistic* conception, and the body of such conceptions as the *dualistic* philosophy. All teleological conceptions are, of necessity, dualistic, just as all causal conceptions are necessarily monistic. The distinction between teleological and theological conceptions vanishes as soon as we class the pantheists among theologists. This class is the great conservative element of mankind, who, looking upon nature as under the control of Omnipotence, logically resign all effort either to do or to know into its hands.

Haeckel also employs the term *dysteleology* in antithesis to teleology, and frequently uses it as a general term to designate the monistic or mechanical philosophy.

The entire body of principles embraced in the Lamarckian, Darwinian, and Haeckelian philosophy, when regarded as having passed through its hypothetical and theoretical stages, takes the form of a science, and receives the very appropriate name, *History of Development (Entwickelungsgeschichte)*, a term adopted by Von Baer and applied to embryonic development, but extended by Haeckel to embrace also the secular development of specific forms. This twofold application of the term History of Development, suggests the natural division of the science into its two great departments. The first of these is essentially that of Von Baer, and treats of the progress of the individual organism from the earliest embryonic condition throughout the numerous successive stages and transformations through which it passes until it arrives at the perfect state. Properly it does not stop at birth, but continues through life, during which, in many creatures, very important metamorphoses take place. This division of the History of Development is denominated *Ontogeny*. The other grand division, which treats of the development of present living forms out of antecedent forms through the influences of heredity (*Vererbung*) and adaptation (*Anpassung*), is termed *Phylogeny*, a term derived from the Greek word φῦλον, a race.

It is to this latter branch of the History of Development that the attention of progressive minds has been heretofore almost exclusively directed, and the arguments of Lamarck and Darwin have been chiefly drawn from considerations of comparative anatomy, of geographical distribution, and of paleontology. The powerful re-enforcement which it has now received from ontogeny was quite unexpected, and the astonishing uniformity with which the ontogenetic facts support, confirm, and corroborate the phylogenetic arguments, may be regarded as having placed the doctrine of development beyond the stage of theory and speculation, and established it as the first law of Biology.

Although the chief facts of ontogeny had been discovered and recorded by Von Baer and others, a quarter of a century before, it was left for Haeckel to first perceive and announce their relation to the law of phylogenetic development, and to urge their irresistible force as arguments for the theory of descent. Von Baer himself, although he had erected them into a "History of Development," seems but dimly to have realized the significance of these embryonic metamorphoses which he has observed and described, and as recently as the date of the late Professor Agassiz' public lectures, is quoted by him in a private letter as still adhering to his doctrine of types, and protesting against that of descent from the apes.[7]

Anthropogeny, or the Genesis of Man, considers all the arguments, both from ontogeny and from phylogeny, in support of the assumption of the descent of the human race in a direct line from the lower animals, shows throughout the length of this line what creatures now existing upon the globe or found fossil in the rocks, stand nearest to this line of descent, and aims to trace the pedigree of the being who is the present undisputed lord of the planet back to the lowest amoeba, and even to the moner. Haeckel does not stop with the ape, with the amphioxus, or even with the ascidian. Guided by the Ariadnean clew of *ontogenesis*, he pursues man's genealogy back through the labyrinth of primordial forms into the cell, and thence still back until he loses it in protoplasm.

Standing, as man does, at the head of the animal kingdom, and forming the last and highest stage of development upon the globe, the history of his progress from the lowest form of organic existence must be co-extensive with that of all other beings. It differs, however, from the history of development in general, in not being concerned with any of the branches that diverge at various points from the main anthropogenetic stem. This becomes obvious when we commence to study phylogeny, but may be noted here as a means of better appreciating the true scope of Anthropogeny. A few illustrations will make it clear.

Not to speak of the entire vegetable kingdom which is lopped off at the first stroke, we find, as we ascend the scale, that one after another the great branches of the Zoophytes, of the Annelids (including all the Articulates and the Echinoderms), of the Mollusca, of the Fishes, of the Reptiles, of the Ungulata and Cetacea, of the Carnivora and Rodentia, and of many other less important groups, are successively passed by and left behind; thus obviating the necessity of following out the special genealogy and development of each of these complicated divisions of natural history. The history of development of man pushes right on, taking such notice only of divergent trunks as is necessary to fix with certainty the position of his line of march.

---

[7] Since the above was written, the death of Von Baer has been announced. His last effort was in the nature of a systematic attack on Darwinism.

II.

ONTOGENESIS.

THE primary law of ontogenesis and that which connects it with the modern theory of development, is founded on the discovery of Von Baer, that the different successive stages of the embryonic development of the higher animals bear a singularly close resemblance to certain lower animals in their adult state, and that the embryos of many animals, and of man himself, in their earlier stages, are scarcely distinguishable from one another. This fact, as already remarked, was carefully studied by Von Baer, and the successive stages of embryonic life systematically compared and co-ordinated. In his great work on the *History of Development of Animals*, (1828-1837), that distinguished embryologist has given to the world the results of his exhaustive investigations. In this work he announces that the theory of types founded by Cuvier in 1816, upon the facts of comparative anatomy, is confirmed by those of embryology, and shows that the process of development, which is the same for all the animals of any of the four types, is different from those of different types.

Haeckel does not gainsay the general truth of this statement, but simply shows that it cannot be used as an argument against the theory of descent, as Von Baer's investigations were confined to fully differentiated animals of each type, and not extended to the then little known Amphioxus and Ascidians, which later researches have shown to constitute transition forms uniting two types. Besides, as we shall see, however different the course of development of different animals may be, the embryos of animals of higher types pass through phases identical with the adult forms of some of the lower types, though not of others, showing that the four types of Cuvier and Von Baer—Radiates, Articulates, Mollusks and Vertebrates—can neither be regarded as co-ordinate, nor as regularly subordinated to each other. And this is not all: Von Baer's own facts, and those of many embryologists, show that there must be another type added to these four; viz. the *Protozoa*, and that from this the course of both phylogenetic and ontogenetic development has been through the Worms directly to the Vertebrates, leaving the remaining types untouched. It seems, therefore, simply that the different branches of the main stem have in our time spread so widely, and become so far differentiated by adaptive influences, that even their embryos have lost many of the original traces of relationship. The important fact remains that within the vertebrate type, as within other types, the embryonic stages correspond with wonderful accuracy to the successively ascending classes and orders established for that type.

The law of Von Baer, expressed in the most general terms, as laid down by himself, is in these words : " The development of an individual of a definite animal form is determined by two relations: first, by a progressive development of the animal body through increasing histological and morphological differentiation (*Sonderung*); secondly, through simultaneous progressive development from a more general form of the type to a more special. The degree of development of the animal body consists in a greater or less amount of heterogeneity of the elementary parts and of the individual components of a composite apparatus; in a word, in the greater histological and morphological differentiation. The type, on the contrary, is the fundamental relation of the organic elements and organs."

Upon this important law, Haeckel puts the new interpretation that the " type " of Von Baer is the representative of the law of *heredity* of Darwin, (the *vis centripeta* of Goethe), while the " degree of development " means neither more nor less than his law of *adaptation* (Goethe's *vis centrifuga*).

The parallelism which is found to exist between the facts of ontogenesis and the facts of phylogenesis, between the embryonic forms of higher, and the adult forms of lower, organisms, is one of the most astonishing discoveries which science has ever made. It is one which would have been least likely ever to be reached by conjecture or by any form of *a priori* reasoning. There was but one possible mode of reaching this truth, and this was by long and patient investigation of the minutest objects and most occult phenomena, without the aid even of a " working hypothesis."

Such a truth must have a meaning. This meaning Von Baer himself never realized and, when pointed out to him by others, never accepted. Yet I venture to predict that no unbiased reader of Haeckel's *Anthropogenie* will any longer doubt the justice of his

conclusions respecting the significance of this marvellous co-inci-
dence. The believers in miracles, who refuse to accept this explanation, will have discovered the most miraculous of all miracles.
The singular alleged action of Providence in stirring fossil shells
and bones into the earth, of which the mountains were made, " as
a cook stirs raisins into a pudding," would be an intelligible phenomenon compared with this. That a man should begin his
existence as an *amoeba*, should subsequently turn into a *worm*, a
little later should become a *lamprey*, later still a fish, and after passing through amphibian, reptilian, monotreme, marsupial, lemurian,
and simian forms, should at last emerge with the human shape,—
this series of remarkable metamorphoses, if required to be explained
on the assumption that it is directed by the arbitrary will of the
Creator, would furnish a more fatal stumbling-block than even
the presence of those useless and usually deleterious rudimentary
organs, which all higher animals are found to possess. For
even if we can bring ourselves to comprehend how the Creator
may, for some inscrutable reason, introduce many arbitrary irregu-
larities into his handiwork, according as he may be actuated by
this or that caprice, we are still at a loss to understand how he
should wish to carry on a whole system of freaks in the embryo,
which have a manifest correspondence with the mature forms of
life known to exist upon the globe, unless there be some causal
connection between the two systems. Nothing short of the most
complete abnegation of reason, nay, of a strong effort to accept
the unreasonable, can prevent the mind, cognizant of these two
series of facts, from becoming thoroughly convinced that such a
dependence must subsist.

The science which embraces both the ontogenetic and the phylogenetic development of life, the genesis of life in general, is called
by Haeckel *Biogenia*, a science, as he remarks, as yet scarcely
founded. The law which expresses the relation between the
facts of ontogeny and the facts of phylogeny is, therefore, the
fundamental law of *biogenia*. Stated in the most direct manner,
this law is that " phylogenesis is the *mechanical cause* of ontogenesis." From a somewhat altered point of view, the same idea is
conveyed by saying that ontogenesis is a *brief recapitulation* of phylogenesis, or, that the history of the *germ (Keimesgeschichte)* is an
abridgment or *epitome* of the history of the *race (Stammesgeschichte)*.

Mathematically enunciated, the germ-development becomes a *function* of the race-development, so that every differentiation of the latter carries with it a corresponding and consequential differentiation of the former. This is the fundamental law of organic development, the great biogenetic ground-principle, to which the student of the history of development, whether of its ontogenetic or its phylogenetic aspect, must continually recur. The law of heredity, which Goethe calls " the stubborn power of permanency in whatever has once possessed reality," while it graciously yields to the influence of surrounding circumstances and admits of progress, nevertheless requires, with all the rigor of sovereignty, that every step forward shall be taken through the established channels, and with due respect for the most ancient forms. The human germ may, indeed, develop and perfect itself in the highest form of organized existence, but the old and time-honored fish-form and worm-form and amoeba-form, nay, even the moner-form, must be respected, and the proud man-germ must humbly bow to the inexorable decree of Nature, and must undergo this manifold and repeated *metempsychosis*, which in its strange reality eclipses all the dreams of Thales and Pythagoras.

Phylogenesis, which is a cause, begins with the moner; ontogenesis, which is a consequence, begins with the cell. For man, as for all animals that have advanced beyond an extremely low stage of existence, there is but one mode by which new individuals of the race can be created and the race itself perpetuated, and that is by the contact of two germinal principles having opposite sexual polarities. Each of these principles is a simple cell. The male is the sperm-cell, the female the germ-cell. Only by the union and literal blending of these two cells can generation take place,

The cell is the lowest organized form of existence. It is also the last term in the histological analysis of the tissues of the body. An animal is ultimately nothing more than an organized assemblage of cells, a compound individual.

The moner is a lower form of existence than the cell, the lowest known form, and may be distinguished as a wholly unorganized and undifferentiated individual.

There are but two essential properties of a cell, a central *nucleus* and surrounding *protoplasm*. The only organization, the only differentiation, is that which distinguishes these two substances. And this is itself very slight. Chemically, they can scarcely be distinguished. Both consist of a carbon compound, containing a certain proportion of nitrogen, and belong to the albuminous group, of which all animal tissues are principally composed. The nucleus is generally of a darker color, but sometimes of a lighter, and may or may not contain in its centre a minute dot—*nucleolus.* It also may or may not be surrounded by a membranous envelope. This is generally present in the cells of plants, while it is generally absent in those animals.

The form of cells differs according to the circumstances of their existence. They are the most plastic and easily modified by external conditions of all organized beings, and therefore make the best subjects for the study of the law of adaptation. Stationary cells in a motionless medium are uniformly spherical. When subjected to pressure they assume hexagonal, elongated, or compressed forms, according to the nature of the pressure. Cells that are active in a liquid medium have a portion of the matter composing their outer parts extended into a caudal appendage away from the direction of motion. In addition to the forms named, cells frequently assume others, sometimes taking wholly amorphous shapes, resulting from the particular conditions to which they may be subjected. They frequently change their form, and this not only from external influences, but in obedience to internal or subjective determinations. For a cell is a living creature. It possesses all the essential characteristics of an organized individual. The only functions necessary to characterize a living being are nutrition and propagation. Both these the cell possesses. It grows by the absorption of nourishment from the medium in which it lives. Where this nourishment is not uniformly mingled throughout the medium, but exists in the form of scattered solid particles, the cell acquires the power to extend portions of its substance into temporary organs of grasping (*pseudopodia*), and thus to enclose and devour its food. It thus improvises a mouth and jaws on whichever side it may need them, and feeds itself after the manner of another animal.

The cell propagates, like many much higher organisms, by division, or fission. It continues to take nourishment and to grow until it reaches the limit fixed by heredity for its size, and then, instead of growing larger or of ceasing to take food, it divides into two distinct cells. Each of these then goes through with the same process of nutrition and division, and so on.

But besides these two essential phenomena, which are common to all life, whether animal or vegetable, the cell performs two other truly animal functions. It possesses the power of *locomotion*, and the faculty of *sensation*. Cells with caudal appendages, called lash-cells (*Geisselzellen*), have acquired that form in consequence of their independent activities in their liquid medium. Various other forms are traceable to similar causes. As a proof of the possession by cells of a faculty of sensation, we have only to consider the efforts of various kinds to obtain their food. Some are actually carnivorous, and show a certain degree of dexterity in capturing their prey. They are, therefore, not only capable of feeling, but, in a qualified sense, of thinking and of reasoning.

There is no essential difference between the sperm-cells and germ-cells of higher animals, and the simple cells of which many lower animals consist, and beyond which they never advance. We can only say that among the infinitely varied forms of life we find that while most creatures have developed into highly compound states, and only revert to the original unicellular condition at the beginning of each individual's existence, there are still many creatures that never progress beyond this primordial stage, and whose entire existence is passed in the form and condition of simple cells.[6] Among such creatures may be named the *Amoebae*, the *Gregarinae*, the *Infusoria*, etc. These animals, as well as those which consist simply of an accumulation or aggregation of cells, such as the *Labyrinthuleae*, etc., and which form the second stage of development, never rising above the cellular condition, are classed by Haeckel, together with his *Planaeada*, in a grand-division or department by themselves, and called *Protozoa*. A further ground for this classification will be seen later.

According to the fundamental biogenetic law above stated, the cell must be the primordial form out of which all more highly organized beings, including man, have developed, since it is the original stage of their ontogenetic development. And as there still exist unicellular beings resembling the sperm-cells and the

[6] A complete description, both popular and systematic, of all the unicellular organisms known to exist, was published by Prof. Haeckel in 1878, entitled *Das Protisten-reich*, of which he has kindly sent the writer a copy.

germ-cells of higher organisms, the deduction is warranted that all higher creatures are the descendants of some form of these unicellular beings. Considering the differences that may and do exist even in cells, and in animals consisting of a single cell, Haeckel is led to the conclusion that of all the unicellular creatures known to science, the *Amœba* bears the strongest evidence of being the original progenitor of the human race.

The history of the discovery of the human *ova* and *spermatozoa* deserves a brief notice. In 1672, De Graaf discovered the Graafian vesicle, which he supposed to be the ovum itself. In 1797, Cruikshank, Prevost and Dumas found and described the true ovules, but failed to comprehend their real nature and importance. It was left for Von Baer, thirty years later, to complete the discovery, and place it before the world in its full light. Pürkinje (1825) and Wagner (1835) added important contributions in the discovery of the germinative vesicle or nucleus, and the germinative dot or *nucleolus*. The fact that the ova are simple cells could not be recognized until after the founding of the universal cell-theory by Schleiden (1838) and Schwann (1839). It was then perceived that eggs themselves are cells, differing in scarcely any respect from the cells of other tissues.

The discovery of the spermatozoa, or male seminal animalcules, was first made by Leeuwenhoek in 1674, and confirmed by Louis Ham in 1677. A long war arose between the so-called *Animalculists* and *Ovulists*, the first of which believed that the animalcules were the true and only germs of the future being, which simply found in the ova a suitable *matrix* for their development, while the latter maintained that the ova were the true germs, which were only affected with a germinative impulse by contact with the spermatozoa. The real nature of this mysterious process has only been clearly brought to light by the labors of more modern investigators, among the foremost of whom must be ranked Prof. Ernst Haeckel, of Jena.

The ova of all mammals are identical in all essential characteristics. They all possess both nucleus and nucleolus, are of a spherical form, and about one-tenth of a line in diameter, and all acquire at maturity a membranous envelope called the *chorion* or *zona pellucida*. The egg of a mouse and that of an elephant cannot be distinguished from each other or from the human ovum in any respect. They are all simple cells.

The sperm-cells of mammals possess a no less marked similarity, They are exceedingly small as compared with the germ-cells, and possess long filiform caudal appendages. The *chorion* is wanting. Their form may be divided into head, body and tail, but between no two of these parts can there be said to exist any clear line of separation. The head contains the nucleus surrounded by protoplasm or cell-substance, which is carried backward in gradually diminished quantity, forming the remaining portions. It was not until the year 1873 that it was discovered that these important organisms, like the female ova, were simple cells. This discovery is in great part due to Prof. Haeckel's own investigations.

We may now consider the immediate consequences of the union of the sperm-cell with the germ-cell. The *spermatozoon* penetrates the many times larger *ovum*, making its entrance through minute pores in the *chorion*, and mingling at once with the germinative matter of the cell. A remarkable change takes place. Two perfect cells with opposite sexual polarities have been drawn together by their inherent affinities. They have met and their substances have commingled. They literally blend into one individual. But that individual is no longer a cell. The sperm-cell has lost its individuality and wholly disappeared. The nucleus of the germ-cell has likewise entirely vanished. The entire interior of the original cell has become a homogeneous mass of protoplasm, no longer possessing any traces of organization. Only the *chorion* remains to determine its original form. It is a case of retrogression (*Rückbildung*), of reversion to the lowest type of existence. The human being who, as represented in sperm-cell and germ-cell, stands on the plane of the *amœba* and the *infusorium*, has gone back, on the union of these cells, to that of the *moner*. As if nature was not satisfied that any form of life should begin with the cell, the second stage of existence, but required absolutely that every being, no matter how high might be its destiny, should go to the very foot of the scale and climb the entire distance, in order that it might pass through every form that has belonged to its whole line of ancestors.

From another point of view, this union and literal blending of the male and female principles is not only of the highest intellectual interest, but is calculated to awaken the most lively æsthetic sentiments. Nothing more poetic or romantic has ever been presented

to the human fancy by all the fictions of the world than the marvellous reality of this courtship of cells! The very fountain-head
of love (*Urquelle der Liebe*)is reached in the affinities of two cells!
The ruling passion of all ages has its ultimate basis in this new-
found physiological fact. When the march of science shall have
exposed the false basis upon which the present artificial code of
social life rests, and when the fears of those who can imagine
nothing better shall have been dispelled, then let the future Homer
of science sing, not the illicit loves of Paris and Helen, which
whelm great nations in untimely ruin, but the lawful wooings
and the heroic sacrifices of the sperm-cell and the germ-cell as
they rush into that embrace which annihilates both that a great
and advancing race may not perish from the earth! And here
there is no fiction, there is not even speculation. Both the plot
and details of this tale belong to the domain of established fact,
and rest upon the most thorough scientific investigation.

The structureless form first assumed by the fecundated ovum is
termed a *cytod*, but from the circumstance of its being the ontogenetic form, which corresponds to the moner, Haeckel has also
applied to it the systematic name of *Monerula*. In his system this
is the stage of germ-development which the moner, before its
further differentiation, had impressed upon all organic matter,
and through which all higher forms must consequently invariably
pass.

This *cytod* or *monerula* stage is, however, of short duration.
Very soon the homogeneous mass acquires a new nucleus, and
thus again assumes the character of a simple cell. This second
cell-form is so similar to that of the unfecundated ovum that many
observers who had actually witnessed the cytod-form, on looking
again, soon after, and seeing only the primary cell-form, had dis-
credited their intermediate observations. It was not until the entire transformation had been repeatedly witnessed through all the
steps of its progress, that the fact of such a strange transition became established beyond a doubt.

The new cell, although indistinguishable from the old, possesses
an invisible element derived from the absorbed substance of the
sperm-cell which gives it the potential character of the parents.
The old cell, as such, was an independent living organism, capable of performing the essential functions of life, including that of

reproducing its kind ; *i. e.*, of dividing up into cells like itself, but which could progress no farther. The new cell, on the other hand, is the germ of a highly-organized being.

This is the *second*, or *ovulum-stage* of development which has been impressed upon the germ by the *amœba* stage of phyloge-netic development. The human being is now an *amœba*.

The next step in the development of the fecundated germ con-sists in a process of division which takes place in the nucleus. This first divides into two, and the surrounding protoplasm ar-ranges itself into two hemispheres so as to form a double cell. Then each of these two nuclei, with its surrounding protoplasm, goes through the same process, dividing the cell into four parts. The same process is then repeated for each of these parts, and so on, increasing the division in a geometrical progression, until the entire contents of the *chorion* consist of a mass of closely-aggregated minute cells.

The form which the fecundated egg has now assumed, is called, from its resemblance to a mulberry, the *Morula*, and constitutes the *third*, or *Morula-stage* of development. It is merely a com-pound form of the simple cell. Instead of one comparatively large cell, it now consists of an aggregated society of small cells. Prof. Haeckel has established a theoretical group of compound amoebæ, which he calls *Synamœbia*, as the phylogenetic ancestral form to which the *Morula* owes its existence; but it has been shown by the researches of Archer and Cienkowski into some species of *Cystophrys* and into the *Labryinthulcæ*, that these hypothetical *Synamœbia* have an actual representation in the fauna of the globe. These creatures are found to consist of formless accumulations of similar simple cells.

The *fourth* stage of germinal development is the *Blastosphacre-stage*. It consists of a transformation of the *Morula*, which is brought about by the absorption of a clear fluid from the medium in which it is situated, which collects at the centre and crowds the cells outward, pressing them together until they are made to form a single layer upon the inner surface of the chorion, and thus leav-ing the whole interior filled only with the new liquid. The germ is enlarged during the process, from its former diameter of about one-tenth of a line to that of half a line. The cells now forming this single layer have assumed a hexagonal shape, due to their

lateral pressure against one another. The new form is denominated the *Blastosphaera* or *vesicula blastodermica*, while the cellular
layer bears the name of *germinal membrane* (*Keimhaut*) or *blasto-
derm*.

The blastosphaere is a stage of embryonic development which is
common to all creatures that have a higher organization than that
of the synamoebian societies of cells. In many of the lower forms
of life it becomes a stage of metamorphosis rather than of embryonic development, since these minute blastosphaeres lead independent lives for a time, as the larvæ of higher forms. This is the case
with the calcareous sponges, with many zoöphytes, worms, ascidians and molluscs. Such larvæ are called *Planulæ*. They are
usually covered with cilia, which serve as aids to locomotion.
These facts alone would justify the believer in the dependence of
ontogeny upon phylogeny in maintaining that this stage had once
formed the highest plane of development, and that there had once
existed a race of creatures which, after passing through the three
preceding stages, completed their career as true blastosphaeres, and
that all higher organisms must, in that sense, be descendants of
such a race. Haeckel assumes such a group of creatures, which
he calls the *Planaeada*. This hypothesis, however, was scarcely
necessary, from the fact that there are animals well known to
science which conform in their general structure entirely to this
stage of development. Many such creatures now exist, both in
the sea and in fresh water, consisting of a single exterior layer of
cells, surrounding a fluid or gelatinous interior, and usually provided, like the larval forms, with locomotive cilia. Especially may
be mentioned the *Synura* in the *Volvocinae* and the *Magosphaera
planula*. The latter was discovered and named by Haeckel, who
has carefully traced its development through the lower stages, and
proved the *Planula* to be its highest and mature condition. Such
an animal is, therefore, a true *Planaea*, as strictly so as are the
members of Haeckel's theoretical ancestral group of *Planaeada*.

To the philosophical embryologist, the blastosphaere-stage presents an extraordinary interest. Nothing could illustrate this
better than the remarkable utterance which it has elicited from Von
Baer himself, one of the few of his statements which possess not
only an ontogenetic, but also a phylogenetic significance. "The
farther we go back," says he, "the greater agreement do we find,

even in the most different animals. We are thus led to the question, whether at the commencement of development, all animals were not essentially alike, and whether there does not exist for all a common primordial form? As the germ is the undeveloped animal itself, so it may be reasonably stated that the simple blasto-sphaere (*Blasenform*) is the common fundamental form out of which all animals are, not only ideally, but historically developed."

The next and *fifth* stage of embryonic development is the most important of all, as it leads us directly to the consideration of Haeckel's celebrated *"Gastraea Theory."* The ontogenetic form is called the *Gastrula*, which differs in two important respects from the *Planula*. Instead of a single cellular layer, as in the latter, the Gastrula possesses two such layers, one immediately within the other. These layers themselves differ from that of the Planula, in consisting of several rows of cells instead of one, thus forming two distinct coats composed each of several layers of cells. These two coatings are quite independent of each other, and may be easily separated, which is not the case with the layers of cells composing each coat. The two coats differ still further from each other, in being made up of unlike cells. Those of the inner are larger, softer, and darker colored than those of the outer.

The other important distinction between the Gastrula and the Planula is the possession by the former of an orifice at one point on its surface, through which it receives its nourishment, and excretes refuse materials. This form of the *Gastrula-stage*, however, it should be stated, cannot be identified in the higher vertebrates. In man it is represented merely by a disc-shaped thickening at one spot on the spherical germ, and the formation there of the two primary germinative layers which extend round into a sort of sack, which is the unmistakable homologue of the typical *Gastrula* of the lower animals.

The process by which the embryo passes from the *Planula* to the *Gastrula* state, though simple, would be somewhat tedious, and the reader must be referred for the details of this transition to treatises on embryology, or to Prof. Haeckel's own work.

An extraordinary interest attaches to this stage of ontogenetic development, in consequence of its carrying the embryo across the line which separates the *Protozoa* from the *Metazoa*. Haeckel insists upon this as the primary division of the animal kingdom.

The *Protozoa* are not a co-ordinate department or type with the Vertebrates, Mollusks, etc. They constitute a sub-kingdom, co-ordinate only with the other sub-kingdom of *Metazoa*, under which these types all fall. To class the *Protozoa* among the Radiates would be equivalent to placing the Cryptogams under the Endogens in a botanical system. The reasons for this are purely ontogenetic. The *Gastrula* possesses the two primary germinative layers, which belong to none of the forms below it. The most thorough embryological research has established beyond a doubt the important fact that all the tissues of the body of every animal that develops beyond that stage, are evolved out of the one or the other of these primary layers. The *Protozoa* and the *Metazoa* are therefore separated by the broadest possible line of demarkation, the former possessing no primary germinative layers, while the latter are either composed of them or developed out of them.

The extreme importance of these cellular layers, therefore, becomes at once apparent, and it is upon the manner in which the different tissues of the body are formed out of this simple building material that the most patient and indefatigable embryologists have been engaged during the past half century. It is found that from the outer layer or *exoderm* are formed : first, the *epidermis* and organs arising from it (hair, nails, feathers, scales, etc.); secondly, the nervous system and the most important part of the organs of sense ; thirdly, the greater part of the flesh of the body, the muscles ; and fourthly, the skeleton of vertebrates ; in short, all the organs of *locomotion* and *sensation*.

Out of the inner layer, or *entoderm*, on the other hand, are developed first, the inner lining or epithelium of the entire cavity of the body, together with that of all the glands and organs belonging to it, lungs, liver, etc. ; secondly, the muscles of the internal vegetative system, including the heart ; and thirdly, the cells of the generative organs. This last, however, is still open to some doubt.

In consequence of these special functions performed by each of the two primary germinative layers, the outer one has been called the animal germ-layer (*animales Keimblatt*), and the inner the vegetative germ-layer (*vegetatives Keimblatt*). The Latin terms *exoderma*, *dermophyllum*, *lamina dermalis*, and *lamina serosa*, have also been applied to the former, and *entoderma*, *gastrophyllum*, *lamina gastralis*, and *lamina mucosa* to the latter.

The *Gastrula* is a common larval form of many lower animals, such as Sponges, Polyps, Corals, Medusae, Worms, Mollusks, and Radiates. It is also a larval form of the two most interesting of all animals for the history of development : viz., the Ascidian and the Amphioxus. Many Zoöphytes and sponges are indeed nothing more in their final state than an aggregation or society of *Gastrulae*. They therefore constitute a compound *Gastraea*.

There is still another larval form belonging to this class which possesses an almost equal interest with the Gastrula. This is the *Ascula*. It belongs to the life histories of both Sponges and Medusae, being developed out of the gastrula-form, and from it the fundamental biogenetic law leads us back to the long extinct *Protascus*, or primordial sack, which was the ancient progenitor of the Zoöphytes. It is fixed to the bottom of the sea, having its open end directed upward. No longer needing the cilia employed by the Gastrula as organs of locomotion, these are consequently wanting. Its body consists of a simple sack or stomach, whose walls are formed by the two primary germinative layers in all their primordial simplicity.

The already famous *Gastraea Theory* of Haeckel is nothing more than the simple application of his fundamental biogenetic law to the Gastrula stage of development. By this law he is led to the conclusion that at one period in the history of the globe, an animal, having at maturity the form and organization of the *Gastrula*, and to which he gives the name of *Gastraea*, constituted the highest form of organic development upon it, and that from this primordial state of the two primary germinative layers, the process of differentiation of organs proceeded, until the present complex state of the animal kingdom has been reached, even as from the embryonic gastrula-form the highest of living beings are now developed through this ontogenetic recapitulation. "The Gastraea," says he, "must have lived at least during the Laurentian period, and sported about in the sea by means of its ciliated exterior coat, in the same manner as the free-moving Gastrulae now do."

The great interest which attaches to the Gastraea Theory, as already remarked, arises out of the immense importance of the primary germ-layers as the basis of all future histological development. That which carries it further out into the field of speculation, however, and thus in one way adds still more to its interest,

is the difficulty both in finding the true homologue in man and
the higher vertebrates generally, of the Gastrula of the Ascidian
and Amphioxus, and also in finding any good systematic representative of the ancestral Gastraea.

The rest of the history of the ontogenetic development of man
is the history of the differentiation of the two primary germinative layers. The Gastrula stage has furnished, in these two layers,
the raw material for the entire future structure. By watching the'
progress of growth in exoderm and entoderm, the successive tissues of every part of the body may be traced to the highest degrees
of specialization. From this point of view that stage possesses an
interest far exceeding that of all those that have preceded it: for in
it is found the first truly specialized organ. That organ is the stomach. The two essential functions of life are nutrition and reproduction. The one is the promoter of ontogenetic, the other of
phylogenetic development. But, as we saw in the cell, these two
functions are originally one, and that one is nutrition. Reproduction appears here as a mere continuation of nutrition. Nutrition
goes on to the limit of growth, when division takes place. Nutrition is commuted into reproduction. *Generation is phylogenetic
nutrition;* a truth which we should never have reached except by
the study of the lowest organisms. Nutrition, therefore is the one
essential function of life. The organ of nutrition is the stomach.
How significant, and yet how reasonable, that in the course of
development the first specialized organ should be the stomach, and
that the first creature possessing a specialized organ should consist
wholly of a stomach! Such a form is the *Gastrula;* such a creature was the *Protascus;* and such is the hypothetical *Gastraea* of
Haeckel.

The *sixth* stage of the ontogenetic development gives the human
embryo the form and organization of a worm. Our moral and
religious teachers have from time immemorial delighted in remind-
ing us that we were but "worms of the dust." They should thank
science for demonstrating that they were right. We might almost
give them credit for an inspirational insight, did they not render
their sincerity questionable by the indignation they evince when
told that in the same sense that we are worms, we are also apes.

The first important step in the progress of embryonic development, after leaving the Gastrula-stage, is the formation of two

additional germ-layers out of the two original ones. The exact mode of their development is still under discussion among embryologists. Haeckel believes that the original exoderm and entoderm secrete each a new layer of cells from its inner surface ; that is, from the surface of each which is contiguous to the other, so that the two new layers lie against each other and separate the primary by the thickness of both. It is, nevertheless, considered that in the process the original constitution and identity of the primary layers are destroyed, so that they have virtually resolved themselves into four secondary germ-layers. The two outer layers, however, now perform together the office of the original exoderm, while the two inner ones take the place of the entoderm. This division into four secondary germinative layers is the final division, all the tissues, without exception, being formed out of these, as they have in nearly every case been traced.

The names assigned by Von Baer and by Haeckel to these secondary layers have reference to the functions which they are found to perform. Being all German in their etymology, they are difficult to render into English. The following may answer as such an imperfect version:—Numbering them from the outside, the first is called by Von Baer the skin or dermal layer (*Hautschicht*), and by Haeckel the dermo-sensory leaf or fold (*Hautssinnesblatt*). The second is the muscular layer (*Fleischschicht*) of Von Baer, and the dermo-fibrous leaf or fold (*Hautfaserblatt*) of Haeckel. The third is Von Baer's vascular layer (*Gefässschicht*), and Haeckel's gastro-fibrous leaf or fold (*Darmfaserblatt*). The fourth, or extreme inner layer, Von Baer has denominated the mucous layer or membrane (*Schleimschicht*), while Haeckel calls it the gastro-glandular leaf or fold (*Darmdrüsenblatt*). Space will admit of no further following out of this interesting part of the history of embryonic development.

All worms are composed of these four secondary germ-layers, the lowest possessing them in their greatest simplicity. The popular idea of a worm is an elongated creature, consisting of many joints or rings (*somites*), but this is only a compound state of the primitive worm, each ring or joint constituting, zoölogically, a distinct individual, and possessing morphologically, if not physiologically, all the characters of one. The primitive worm has but one joint. Among the lowest of the worms are the *Turbellaria*, which in many respects resemble the *Gastrulae* of some higher animals. Like them, their body consists of a simple sack with only a single orifice, and even possesses the ciliary organs of locomotion. The great difference lies in the nature of the cellular layers composing this sack. In the *Turbellaria* these-are the four secondary instead of the two primary germinative layers. Haeckel reasons here to an ancient primordial worm (*Urwurm*, *Prothelmis*), corresponding, in all respects, with this stage of embryonic development in man and the higher animals generally, and from which not only all other worms, but all creatures higher than the worms, including mankind, have descended. This worm-stage acquires an increased interest from the circumstance that here the main trunk divides, sending off the articulate branch in one direction and the mollusk branch in another, leaving only the vertebrate stem. The embryo assumes a certain bilateralness, the four secondary germinative layers grow together at their dorsal median line, and a *chorda dorsalis* is formed. This is the true *Chordonium-stage*. The embryo now has the closest affinities with the larval state of the Ascidian, which, strangely enough, though wholly devoid of a *chorda* in its final state, has a well-defined one in its larval state. There is another creature, the *Appendicularia*, which possesses a *chorda dorsalis* throughout its existence, although in all other respects it is a true worm, and belongs, with the ascidians, to the *Tunicata*. This animal is the true connecting link between the worms and the vertebrates, between the ascidian and the amphioxus. The hypothetical *Chordonium* of Haeckel, the assumed ancestor of the human race at this stage, and exact representative of the embryo at this period of its growth, differs scarcely at all from the *Appendicularia*. It is the common ancestor of the *Tunicata* and the *Vertebrata*.

From a worm, the embryo passes directly into a vertebrate. As the ascidian larvæ, the appendicularia, and the amphioxus are separated only by the smallest differences, although the two former are clearly worms, while the latter is clearly a vertebrate, so the corresponding transition stages in the embryo are distinguished only by almost imperceptible shades.

The future man is now a vertebrate, but without distinct vertebræ. He is wholly without brain or cranial enlargement, without a regular heart, without mouth, without limbs. He now belongs to a great subtype of the *Vertebrata*, which Haeckel denominates the *Acrania.* This entire sub-type has now but a single known living representative on the globe, the amphioxus[9]; but Haeckel believes that a period existed when the *Acrania* greatly prevailed over the *Craniota*, or cranium-bearing vertebrates, and peopled all the seas and waters. This *Acrania* or amphioxus form constitutes the *seventh* stage of ontogenetic development.

The next or *eighth* stage is the *Lamprey* or *Monorrhina stage.* The nervous system and the vertebral column begin to differentiate. The spinal marrow undergoes a slight enlargement at its anterior extremity, which is the rudiment of the brain. The vertebral column begins to develop out of the rudimentary *chorda dorsalis.* This does not take place by a gradual, simultaneous formation of all the vertebræ along the line of the *chorda*, but, singular as it may seem, by the formation of one vertebra after another, beginning with the most anterior. This remarkable process points unmistakably to the composite character of the frame-work of every vertebrate body. Each vertebra of a vertebrate, like each ring of an annelid, represents a distinct and once independent unit of a compound organism.

The present *Cyclostomata* or *Monorrhinae* are believed by Haeckel to be the sparse remains of a once great group of animals, which in ancient times shared the possession of the globe with their gradually increasing rivals, the *Amphirrhinae*, which had sprung from them just as the embryo of every higher vertebrate passes from the condition of the one into that of the other. The type of the former is the still living Lamprey or *Petromyzon.* As the names imply, the *Monorrhinae* have but one orifice for mouth and nose, which is of a circular shape, and is used as a sucker, while the *Amphirrhinae* are provided with a pair of jaws and two nasal orifices. Excluding the Amphioxus (*Acrania*) the entire vertebrate type (*Craniota*) falls under these two groups, the *Amphirrhinae* embracing all the higher vertebrates, from the lower fishes upward.

From the form of the first of these groups to that of the second the embryo now passes, and enters upon its *ninth* stage of development; it becomes a fish. But as *natura non facit saltum*, this first

[9] A second acranial animal, discovered near Peale Island, Morton Bay, Australia, has very recently been reported to the Royal Society by Prof. W. Peters, who has described it under the name of *Epigomethys cultellus.* This discovery is of the highest interest to naturalists.

fish-form is not that of a true *Teleost*, or ordinary bony fish, but of a *Selachian*. Indeed, the higher fish-form is never attained, but the embryo skims along at the bases of the great ichthyic and amphibian branches, without becoming at any time a true fish or a true Batrachian. This is a very significant fact, and one which, while it is easily accounted for by the general theory of descent, forms at the same time a powerful ontogenetic argument for the truth of that theory. For the typical representatives of any great group exhibit only the extremities of greatly differentiated branches remote from the parent stem, and it is not to be expected that in the corresponding embryonic forms of animals higher up the stem we should see anything but copies of those forms which existed prior to, or at the commencement of, ramification, and which are consequently within the common line of descent of both.

Some will, perhaps, regret that their ancestors should have been worms, while they cannot count in their pedigree either the bee or the ant; others may not feel flattered to be informed of their close relationship with the frog and the toad; but few, I think, will be sorry to learn that their forefathers were not reptiles, though this fact precludes the more pleasant thought of claiming relationship with the birds; for birds, with all their grace, beauty, and innocence, are neither more nor less than transformed reptiles.

The human embryo passes along the base of the Batrachian branch and through the *Sozura* (thus saving its tail) and so keeps quite aloof from the whole race of lizards, snakes, turtles, etc., and *à fortiori*, of birds. The unborn man is first a Selachian, then a Lepidosiren, then a Siren, and finally a Triton. His first limbs are fins, his first respiratory organs are gills, and his lungs are at first fish-bladders.

The *tenth* and last stage of ontogenetic progress is denominated by Haeckel the *Amnion-stage*. This stage embraces not only that of all true mammalian forms, but also takes in the two interesting antecedent groups, the *Monotremata* and the *Marsupialia*. Haeckel establishes a hypothetical *Protamnion*, which he locates in the Permian period, and which he claims to have been the original progenitor of all the *Amniota*, or amnion-bearing animals. The distinguishing characteristic of this embryonic form, as the name implies, is the beginning of the development of the important organ known as the *amnion*, which is simply a large extension of the yolk-sack, and is filled with a nourishing fluid. This fluid is gradually absorbed and appropriated by the embryo, and furnishes a portion of its nutrition. Simultaneously with the amnion is developed also another important organ, the *Allantoïs*, or primordial urinary sack. Both these organs are confined to the three highest classes of Vertebrates (reptiles, birds and mammals). The embryo now begins to manifest decided mammalian characteristics. Already, the gills have disappeared, having become transformed into jaws, hyoid bones, and otolithes: the heart has acquired its four chambers, and the swim-bladders have been specialized into lungs. For a while the uro-genital and excrementary orifices empty into the common *cloaca* giving it the *monotreme* character. Then, while the allantoïs is still present, a partition separates these, making both open externally. This is the Marsupial stage. Lastly, the allantoïs is transformed into a *placenta*, and the pure mammalian stage is reached. Leaving the great branches of the *Carnivora* and *Rodentia* on the one hand, and of the *Ungulata* and *Cetacea* on the other, the embryo now passes through the various phases of a Sloth-form, an Ape-form, and an Anthropoid-form ; and, conditions being normal, emerges on the two hundred and eightieth day of gestation with the form of a human being.

No one who experiences the least regard for natural truth, whatever views he may hold respecting the meaning of particular facts, can contemplate so remarkable a series of phenomena as this, and realize that he has himself once been the subject of such a strange course of development, without being led into a train of reflection which will open up to his mind broader and juster conceptions of the universe.

At the same time it would be impossible to exaggerate the degree of added strength which a popular acquaintance with the bare facts of ontogenesis would impart to the hypothesis of development or modern doctrine of descent, and thus indirectly to the general conception of the law of universal evolution.

III.

PHYLOGENESIS.

THE fundamental biogenetic law that ontogenesis is an abridged repetition of phylogenesis, that the transformations through which the individual passes during its ante-natal and post-natal existence in the brief period of its career, are a mere reflection of those through which its race has passed during the long ages of its slow development, and that the latter process is the strict physical and mechanical cause of the former,—this deepest of all biological laws Haeckel no longer treats as a *theorem* requiring demonstration, but employs it as a *postulate* by the aid of which all the most troublesome gaps left in the anthropogenetic series by the evidences of comparative anatomy, paleontology, and geographical distribution (*chorology*), are satisfactorily closed. Such gaps have existed along the entire line, rendering it difficult and in many cases impossible to trace it, and leaving so large a part of the whole theory of descent a matter of conjecture, that it was easy for those so disposed to point out unanswerable objections. But once admit the facts of ontogenesis, and miracle alone, and this of the most incredible kind, is the only alternative to the acceptance of the fundamental law, which, candidly viewed in the light of these facts, bears every mark of inherent probability. Not only does this law fill out numerous voids and supply many wholly "missing links" in the phylogenetic chain, but it also confirms, in the most remarkable manner, nearly every item of the evidence furnished by the other sources of proof of the doctrine of descent.

Great, indeed, was the step which this doctrine took when the remarkable revelation was made in the domain of comparative anatomy, that the Amphioxus possessed a *chorda dorsalis*, and that the Ascidian larva contained an even more distinct trace or rudiment of a vertebral column. Professional naturalists, without preconceived ideas could no longer resist the inference that here was the true *nexus* between the worms and the vertebrates. Consider now, the almost crucial verification which this hypothesis received when it was found that the embryonic stages of every creature higher in the scale of being than the Amphioxus presents phases identical with those of that animal and of the Ascidiae, that even the human embryo has its worm-stage immediately succeeded by its Chordonium stage, and this again by its Acranial stage ; the collateral proofs extending even to the germinative layers, and thus rendering the correspondence complete and the inference irresistible. Equally pointed illustrations might be drawn from many other points along the line of common descent.

But valuable as is this class of evidence at these comparatively advanced stages, it is still more so far down toward the dawn of organic existence. For while in the former it only serves to supply the omissions or verify the testimony of an array of paleontological, anatomical, and chorological facts, in the latter it stands alone as the sole evidence of a tangible character of the development of living forms out of the primordial and unorganized *plasma* of nature, and indeed from inorganic matter itself. These ontogenetic stages have already been considered, and unavoidable mention made of many of the forms to which they correspond, and whose stamp they bear.

The deeper problem of the origin of life on the globe is one which strictly belongs to phylogeny, and one which Haeckel has not hesitated squarely and boldly to meet. The doctrine of spontaneous generation, or *archigonia*, is by no means so simple as many suppose, and is not to be settled either by the success or failure to originate bacteria, diatoms, and monads, under certain conditions, in organic infusions.

The only form of generation which has ever yet come within the scope of human observation, and which, from the nature of things, can ever be expected to be directly witnessed by human eyes, is, of course, that wherein the offspring proceeds directly from a known and distinct parentage. This form of generation is called *tocogonia*, and genesis itself in its widest sense is, therefore, primarily divided into *archigonia* and *tocogonia*.

The exceedingly complicated subdivision of tocogonia must be passed over, as we need consider here only the simpler but still somewhat complex one of archigonia, or original spontaneous generation. Although nothing is perhaps empirically known respecting this process, its existence as forming the first link in the phylogenetic chain, possesses the highest degree of probability à *priori*, which is not at all lessened by any empirical failures to subject it to the testimony of the senses.

The problem divides itself into two, which Haeckel considers distinct and independent. The phenomenon assumed by the one he calls *plasmogonia*, in which the genetic process is conceived as taking place in a fluid containing organic matter, which is supposed by some to be essential to the origination of life. The other form of archigonia, on the other hand, conceives the process as taking place in a medium consisting wholly of inorganic elements, and Haeckel accordingly denominates this process *autogonia, i. c.*, unaided self-generation. It will be observed that the great majority of the experiments thus far tried, have been confined to the first of these classes, or plasmogonia. If we now consider the second class, or autogonia, we perceive that this also presents a two-fold problem. It is either a process which, under certain rare and favorable conditions, is going on at all times in some parts of Nature's domains, or it may be one which was only capable of taking place at one period in the geological history of the globe, when conditions existed which were quite different from those now existing, and that all the life now found on the globe has descended through the tocogonic process from the primordial organisms then created.

To all these questions but one answer can be given; but this is an answer which either must be given, or else the whole monistic theory must be surrendered. The answer is that *somewhere and at some time the organic world must have developed out of the inorganic.*

This is all we really *know*, but this we do know just as well as we know that the surface of the earth has undergone the changes which geology teaches that it has undergone. One of three things is certain : either organic life must have existed from eternity, or it must have been created specially, or it must have had a natural origin out of inorganic matter. The first of these contradicts all the facts of geology and all our modern ideas of the cosmogony of our system. The choice lies, therefore, between the other two, and for the consistent dysteleologist there remains no alternative.

Haeckel, however, is undoubtedly too hasty in many of his sweeping assumptions respecting this problem, as for example, that of the direct autogonia of his moners, such as *Bathybius Haeckelii* of Huxley, who dredged it from the bottom of the Atlantic, where it exists in vast quantities as a strange, unorganized mass of living protoplasm. Even this would doubtless be too great a *saltus* for Nature to make. It is certainly far more in harmony with Nature's processes generally, and with the whole tenor of the monistic or genetic philosophy, to conceive that between the two divisions of archigonia which he establishes, autogonia and plasmogonia, there is in Nature a regular gradation, as throughout the rest of her domain, and that she first develops the plasma, that is, some combination of organic matter, consisting of the necessary nitrogenized and carbon compounds in a high state of complexity and instability, and then, as a mere continuation of a uniform pro-cess, impresses this, first with the lowest and then with higher and still higher vital properties. For life is unquestionably a product of molecular organization.

While, therefore, inorganic matter must be regarded as the primordial ancestor of all organized beings, the first stage in the genealogical development of all living things, and hence also of man, must have been some form of *moner*. Haeckel enumerates eight genera of moners now existing on the globe, and there can be no doubt that there are many more still undiscovered, and their extreme and absolutely structureless simplicity renders it highly probable that they are really the first form of life which was developed on the globe.

The direct descendants of the moners are undoubtedly the various forms of *amœba*. About the only observable differentia-tion required to effect this transformation, is the development of a nucleus in the interior of the protoplasmic substance of the former creature. This change converts the *cytod* into a true *cell*, and such is the character of the amoeba, a simple individual of the first order. According to Haeckel, neither the moner nor the amoeba can be strictly classed either with animals or with plants. They belong, together with many other lowly-organized beings, such as the *Flagellata* or lash-cells, the diatoms and the rhizopods, to his famous *third kingdom* the *Protista*. As moners, however, are the lowest of all forms of life, he divides these into three classes, animal moners, vegetable moners, and neutral moners. The first class develop into the lowest animal form, the *Protozoa ;* the sec-ond into the lowest vegetable form, the *Protophyta ;* and the third into the neutral form, the *Protista*. He also speaks of animal amœbæ, and seems to regard these creatures more nearly allied to animals than to plants. At least, he places both the moner and the amœbæ at the base of the animal scale, as the *first* and *second* terms of the phylogenetic series.

From the amoeba-group proceed the true Protozoa, which, therefore, stand in the anthropogenetic line. Applying now the biogenetic law to the *Morula-stage* of ontogenesis, we are able to conclude that these animal amoebas, at one period in their his-tory of development, formed societies or compound individuals

(*Synamoebia*), which therefore constituted the corresponding *third* stage of development in the anthropogenetic line.

There must have next existed, as the *fourth* stage, a family of creatures standing at the base of the protozoa, whose bodies consisted of a simple, hollow sphere, the walls of which were formed of a single layer of cells. These were the *Planaeada*, and they find their embryonic recapitulation in the blastosphaere stage. These creatures are not yet so far extinct but that representatives of them still exist in Haeckel's *Mogosphaera*, in *Synura*, and in other marine and fresh-water forms.

The gastrula-form of embryonic development, barely traceable in the higher vertebrates, but common to both Amphioxus and Ascidiae, as well as to many lower forms, is all there is to warrant the assumption of a class of beings once peopling the waters of the globe, whose bodies consisted of a simple sack, open at one end, and formed of two cellular layers. These were the interesting *Gastraeada*, which have given to all the forms that have descended from them the warp and woof of all their tissues, the primary germinative layers. They must have developed directly out of the *Planaeada*, and form the *fifth* stage in the descent of man.

Ontogenesis next points, as a *sixth* stage, to an extinct race of primordial worms, *Archelminthes*, which originated from the Gastraeada by the formation of an intermediary germinative layer, from which the two inner secondary layers eventually differentiated. These creatures belonged to the lowest sub-division of the worms, the *Acoelomi*, which, as their name implies, possess no cavity of the body (*coelom*) distinct from the sack-like stomach. They are also without any vascular system, heart, or blood, but manifest the first traces of the formation of a nervous system, the simplest organs of sense, and rudiments of secretive and reproductive organs. The typical representatives of the *Archelminthes* are the *Turbellaria*, but they also closely resembled the parasitic Trematoda and Cestoda, which belong to the group *Acoelomi*. Thus is man connected by blood relationship with the loathsome tapeworm that infests his stomach!

Out of the *Acoelomi* were developed the *Coelomati*, which, still low in the scale, nevertheless possess a distinct *coelom*. The now extinct race which effected this transition have been called the *Scolecida*, and form the *seventh* stage of anthropogenetic development. The precise interval which they seem to have bridged over lay between the *Turbellaria* and the *Enteropneusta*, the last of which are represented by the well-known *Balanoglossus*. From this point the great articulate branch swung off, and a little higher the important branch of the Mollusks.

To arrive at the *eighth* stage, we are again compelled to resort to the fundamental biogenetic law, and reason from the chordonium stage of embryonic development of all vertebrates to an extinct form, which must have possessed the rudiment of a vertebral column in the form of a *chorda dorsalis* as a permanent character of its adult state. It would have been wholly impossible to say whether this assumed creature should be placed in the department of articulates, mollusks or worms, were it not for the flood of light which the anatomy of the Amphioxus and the Ascidian has, within the past few years, shed upon the whole problem.

The existence of such a *chorda* in the former of these animals, and its presence also in the larval forms of the latter, are two facts which point unmistakably to the type *Vermes* as the one which has furnished the transition to the *Vertebrata*. No creatures have been found in any of the other types which afford the least intimation of any such transition, and neither in the Protozoa, the Zoöphytes, the Echinodermata, the Crustacea, the Arthropoda, nor the Mollusca, has any trace of a *chorda dorsalis*, either in the larval or adult state, been detected after the most thorough examination. The conclusion is, therefore, irresistible, that the sub-kingdom Vermes and the class *Tunicata* have furnished the true progenitor of the vertebrates. This transition form itself has probably long been extinct, but it has left lineal representatives in the Ascidia, Phallusia, etc., which, while through long adaptation to a fixed existence during their adult state they have lost their *chorda*, still retain that distinctive character during their free larval state, as the unquestionable ontogenetic representative of an organ which they have inherited from their extinct chorda-bearing ancestor. This ancient and primordial ancestor of the vertebrate sub-kingdom to which so many facts, both of ontogenesis and of phylogenesis, with so great certainty point, Haeckel denominates the *Chordonium*. As if to put the solution of this important question beyond the possibility of a future doubt, it is now found that a member of this same group, the *Appendicularia*, actually preserves its chorda during life, and this creature may therefore be regarded as a living representative of the true *Chordonium.*

The Amphioxus forms the *ninth* stage in the anthropogenetic line, and furnishes the first link in the vertebrate chain. It is the only known representative of the once great subdivision of vertebrates called by Haeckel the *Acrania*, or skulless vertebrates.[10] Of this wholly unique and extremely interesting creature sufficient mention has already been made.

The *tenth* stage is that of the *Monorhina*, or *Cyclostoma*, which have for their best-known representative the *Petromyzon* or lamprey. These arose out of the Acrania through a simple enlargement of the anterior extremity of the spinal nerve and the differentiation of the corresponding part of the *chorda dorsalis* into a rudimentary cranium. The distinctive circular mouth-orifice Haeckel regards as a mere adaptive character not present in the original progenitor of the *Craniota.*

The transition to the *eleventh*, the Selachian or primordial fish-stage, took place through the formation of a pair of nostrils and a pair of jaws out of the simple, circular mouth-orifice of the *Cyclostoma*. This transformation led to the *Amphirhina*, a branch of the *Craniota*, systematically coördinate with the *Monorhina*, but embracing all the rest of the vertebrate sub-kingdom. With the higher fishes (*Ganoides* and *Teleostei*) human genealogy is not immediately concerned, but only with the lowest sub-class, the *Selachii*, whose present living representatives are few, and comprise the sharks, rays, etc., but which formed, in the Devonian age, the chief population of the waters of the globe, as their singular heterocercal remains, found in the rocks of that period, abundantly attest.

The transition from the Selachians was next to the *Dipneusta,* which constitute the *twelfth* stage. It was brought about by the natural adaptation of the organs of the body to a partially terrestrial existence. The swim-bladders were transformed into imperfect lungs, the nasal orifices, which in fishes have no communication with the interior of the mouth, established such a communication, and the single auricle of the heart divided into two, thus correspondingly improving the circulation of the blood. The *Dipneusta* therefore employed their gills, which they retained, when in the water, but breathed through their lungs when on land. They form, therefore, a very anomalous and interesting transition group, connecting the lowest fishes with the lowest amphibians. They were a very large class in paleolithic time, as their dental remains testify, but at present only three genera are known, each with a single species, viz :—*Protopterus annectens*, of the rivers of Africa; *Lepidosiren paradoxa*, of tropical America; and *Ceratodus Forsteri*, from South Australian swamps.

Gegenbaur has demonstrated that the real character of the fins of fishes is that of many-toed feet. The changes that led from the fish to the Dipneusta seem not to have affected the number of these toes, although a certain adaptation of the fins to terrestial locomotion was perceptible. The next important transformation was to concern this part of the animal anatomy. The animals nearest related to the Dipneusta are unquestionably the amphibians, with which the former are frequently classed; but they differ from them in the important respect of possessing regular, five-toed feet. But one conclusion can be drawn from this fact, and this is that among the many and varied forms of the once great Dipneusta class, there was one whose locomotive organs had become transformed through adaptation and natural selection into five-toed feet, and that from this long extinct five-toed progenitor, the present amphibians have descended. The human embryo itself, and that of all the higher vertebrates, pass through an analogous transition.

With frogs, toads, and other higher amphibians, as we are most familiar with them, the anthropogenetic line has no direct connection. It constantly hugs the base of the whole group, exhibiting direct relationships only with the *Sozobranchia*, which, therefore, form the *thirteenth*, and the *Sozura*, which form the *fourteenth* stage.

The former of these sub-classes comprises the *Proteus*, the *Siren*, and the *Siredon*, as among its best-known representatives, while to the latter belong the Triton and the Salamander. These once abundant but now comparatively rare creatures have furnished naturalists with some of the most interesting examples of what may almost be called the *visible transmutation of species*. It is well known that frogs and toads (*Anura*), the more highly differentiated amphibians, instead of possessing both lungs and gills.

during life, as do the Dipneusta, undergo a complete metamorphosis after birth, passing from a true fish-form, in the tadpole
state (in which, in addition to the well-known external fish-like
characters, they also possess gills and no lungs and a corresponding piscine circulation) to the familiar batrachian form, in which
their respiration is through lungs only and their circulation through
two auricles. Now, the two sub-classes above named furnish the
most perfect and characteristic transition stages between the larval
and adult stages of the higher amphibians. The Sozobranchia, as
the term implies, preserve their gills through life, but also acquire
lungs, and are therefore strictly amphibious. They live, however,
chiefly in the water, and there perform all the functions of their
existence. The greatest excitement in scientific circles has been
recently called forth by the extraordinary conduct of a member of
this group. The Mexican Axolotl (*Siredon pisciforme*) was observed
in the Paris *Jardin des Plantes*, where large numbers of these
creatures were kept, to frequently take to the land, and several
individuals so far habituated themselves to terrestial life that they
actually lost their gills in the manner of the higher amphibians.
Individuals thus behaving were scarcely distinguishable from the
Amblystoma, a genus of the Sozura which acquire lungs.

An equally remarkable phenomenon, but of exactly the opposite
class, was manifested by the Triton, which belongs to the last
named sub-class, and therefore habitually undergoes the metamorphosis common to frogs, etc., only without the loss of the tail.
Before it arrives at maturity, the Triton, under ordinary circumstances, loses its gills and leads a sub-terrestrial life, breathing
only air. But by placing it in a tank so shaped that it was unable
to get out of the water, it was thus compelled to retain its gills
through life, and even propagated in the water.

All animals above the amphibians are characterized by the possession, during their embryonic stages, of the important organ called
the *amnion*, which is wanting in all below them, and in the amphibians themselves. The facts of ontogenesis, as well as those of comparative anatomy, justify the assumption of the former existence,
probably in the beginning of the Mesozoic age, of a lizard-like
animal whose fossil remains have not yet been discovered, and
whose affinities with any known living form are not close, but
which must have been the first to develop this particular organ,

and was thus the progenitor of all that now possess it, and hence of man himself. This creature, which forms the *fifteenth* stage of man's genealogy, Haeckel calls the *Protamnion*. Out of it was developed primarily the great reptilian class, from which proceeded later the birds, with neither of which has man any direct connection. The origin of the mammals, however, must also be sought in the *Protamnion* stock, from which this class, too, must have proceeded,—perhaps simultaneously with the reptilian branch, though in quite a different direction. The skull of all reptiles and birds is articulated to the atlas by means of a single condyle, while in mammals this condyle is double. From this circumstance the reptiles and birds have been designated by the common term *Monocondylia.* In them, also, the lower jaw is composed of several pieces, and movably joined with the skull by a special process, while in the mammals it consists only of a pair of pieces, and is immediately connected with the temporal bone. The further distinction between the scales and feathers of the former and the hairs of the latter, is likewise an important one. The complete diaphragm of mammals, dividing the thoracic entirely from the abdominal viscera, and which is only partial in the *Monocondylia,* is a further very characteristic distinction. Finally, the existence of mammary glands in the latter, from which the class takes its name, and which are wanting in all other creatures, not only indicates a very distinct position for the mammals, but combines with other characters to place them at the head of the animal series.

A very distinct race, which Haeckel styles the *Promammalia,* forming the next or *sixteenth* stage of man's descent, must have developed out of the *Protamnia,* and transmitted all these marked peculiarities to the entire mammalian class. Man himself possesses all these special mammalian characteristics, and is therefore a genuine mammal.

The nearest known living representative of these hypothetical *Promammalia* are the curious and remarkable *Monotremata* of Australia and Tasmania. Of the entire sub-class only three forms are known, the singular *Orinthorhynchus paradoxus* and the *Echidna,* of which there are two species, *E. hystrix* and *E. setosa.* These animals seem, at first sight, to form an immediate connecting link between the birds and the mammals, as they possess the beak of the former with the lacteal glands of the latter. They further agree with the birds in having the anterior extremities of the clavicles united to the sternum, forming a sort of merrythought. A still more fundamental point of resemblance to the birds, and that from which the sub-class takes its name, is the possession of a common *cloaca*. the urino-genital duct opening within the body. The monotremes, however, agree with the mammals in all the characteristic attributes above enumerated, such as double occipital condyle, complete diaphragm, etc., while the cloaca, the merry-thought, and other apparently avian characters, may have been inherited as well from the amphibians as from the birds. The beak, however, can only be accounted for as having developed independently from adaptation to conditions of existence similar to those which evolved the toothless jaws of turtles, from which it is believed the beak of birds has been derived. The beak of the *Echidna* differs from that of the *Ornithorhynchus*, and exhibits an approach towards the snout of the ant-eaters. The beaks of monotremes and of birds must therefore be regarded as simply analogous, and not as homologous organs.

The Promammalia no doubt differed in many respects from the Monotremata, and Haeckel is inclined to believe that they pos-sessed regular teeth, which the latter lost through adaptive modifi-cation. At least, the earliest fossil remains that paleontologists have been able to refer with certainty to the mammals, and which occur in the triassic formation, consist of teeth only. From a few small molar teeth found in Germany, and also in England, *Micro-lestes antiquus* has been constructed; and from similar dental remains found in this country, *Dromatherium sylvestre* has been described.

Although the Monotremata differ from the *Monocondylia* (rep-tiles and birds) in so many important respects in which they agree with the higher mammals, they, nevertheless, also present many points of difference with these latter. In addition to those already mentioned (cloaca, united claviculæ, etc.), the absence in these animals of any teats upon the mammary glands is very peculiar and anomalous. In consequence of this omission, the only way in which the young are able to obtain their nourishment, is by a process of licking against the porous breast of the mother; and Haeckel, therefore, proposes as a synonym for the ordinary name of the sub-class, that of *Amasta*,—or mammals without teats.

Again, the *allantois* is never transformed into a placenta, the *corpus callosum* is not developed, and there exists a pair of rudimentary marsupial bones. This last character affords almost conclusive proof of the descent of the marsupials from the monotremes.

The *Marsupialia* must therefore be regarded as the next group of animals in the regular line of descent which terminates in man, and as forming the *seventeenth* stage in the development of the human race. Here the cloaca is divided by a horizontal partition into two distinct orifices, both opening externally; nipples are formed on the *mammae*, to which the young attach themselves, and the clavicles are distinct from the sternum. In these respects, the marsupials agree with all the higher mammals. The distinguishing character in which they differ from them, and that from which the name of the sub-class has been taken, is the existence of a remarkable pouch or sack (*marsupium*) on the under side of the female, in which the young are placed at a very early period, and there retained until they are able to take care of themselves. This pouch has been aptly likened to a second or supplementary uterus, and the marsupials have accordingly been called by some *Didelphia*. Our well-known opossum (*Didelphys opossum*) is our only North American representative; but in Australia, this group of animals constitutes the greater part of the mammalian fauna.

The absence of a placenta is the only other important particular in which the marsupials differ from the higher mammals. Indeed, the marsupium seems to constitute a sort of substitute for a placenta, and the want of the latter may be regarded as the physiological cause of the development of the former. The monotremes, however, are without either, and those who know would do well to explain how these animals are able to dispense with them both.

The so-called true *Mammalia* all possess a fully developed placenta, and are therefore distinguished from the two groups last mentioned as forming a third sub-class, the *Placentalia*. This organ is of great importance in the classification of the higher mammals, its mode of attachment furnishing excellent and reliable general characters. In some, for example, the placenta is deciduous from the inner wall of the uterus, while in others it is not, and on this distinction is based the primary division of the whole sub-class into the *Deciduata* and the *Indecidua*. The latter are the least perfectly organized, and comprise the Edentata, the Cetacea, and the Ungulata.   In man the placenta is deciduous, and he can therefore have descended from none of these.

The *Deciduata* again fall into two divisions according as the embryo is attached by the placenta to the uterus upon a single small area or disk, or by a band or girdle extending entirely around it. The former are called *Discoplacentalia*, the latter *Zono-placentalia*. The *Zonoplacentalia* embrace the *Carnaria* (*Carnivora* and *Pinnipedia*) and the *Chelophora*, to which the elephant belongs. The *Discoplacentalia* comprise the rodents, the *Insectivora* (moles, etc.), the *Chiroptera* (bats), the lemurs (*Prosimiae*), and the apes (*Simiae*). To this last legion, also, belongs man, who differs in this respect not at all from the mouse, mole, bat, lemur, or ape.

Now it is a remarkable fact that in one order of the marsupials, the *Pedimana*, embracing the two families *Chironectida* and *Didel-phyida*, to the last of which our opossum belongs, the hind feet are modified, in a peculiar way, into organs for grasping, resembling hands. This group can therefore only be regarded as exhibiting the earliest marks of that important course of transformation which culminated in the apes and in man. The course of development was from this group of marsupials directly to one within the *Deciduata*. Leaving all other animals wholly out of its course, the line of descent of man passes immediately from the *Marsupialia* to the *Prosimiae* or lemur group, an order which Haeckel takes out of Blumenbach's *Quadrumana*, because it is so much farther sepa-rated from the other apes than any of these are from one another. They are ape-like creatures, but shade off in a very interesting way into nearly all the remaining orders of the *Discoplacentalia*. The *Chiromys Madagascariensis* forms the transition to the rodents; the *Galeopithecus* of the Sunda Islands, to the bats; the *Macrotarsi*, to the insectivora; and the *Brachytarsi*, particularly the Lori (*Stenops*), to the true apes. They also exhibit close affinities to the Sloths (*Bradipoda*), which have been regarded as an order of the *Edentata* in the Indecidua ; but recent investigations have proved that they have a deciduous placenta, and therefore it must be at this point that the Deciduata and the Indecidua join.   The lemurs are harmless and melancholy nocturnal animals of a graceful form, and are chiefly confined to the islands south of Asia and east of Africa, and particularly to Madagascar. Their frequency on the islands of the Indian Ocean led the English naturalist Sclater to name this once continental, but now mostly submerged region, *Lemuria*, a circumstance to which Haeckel has given special prominence, by pointing out the many facts which conspire to justify us in the conjecture that here may have existed the true "cradle of the human race." The lemurs form the *eighteenth* stage in the anthropogenetic line.

From the lemurs to the true apes, the transition is comparatively easy. They evidently developed out of the *Brachytarsi,* the *Stenops* forming the nearest approach to a connecting link.

Linnæus, with almost prophetic ken, notwithstanding his dualistic proclivites, classed man with the apes, lemurs, and bats, in his celebrated order, Primates. Blumenbach fancied he saw in the human foot a pretext for rescuing man from this association, and accordingly erected for him a separate order, which he called *Bimana* (two-handed), distinguishing the apes, etc., as *Quadrumana* (four-handed). This classification was adopted by Cuvier, and is the one which has generally prevailed among naturalists, down to Huxley and Haeckel. Huxley, however, gave the whole subject a complete re-investigation, and arrived at the conclusion that Blumenbach's order *Bimana* cannot be maintained on anatomical grounds. He shows, in the most convincing manner, that the distinctions alleged to exist between the posterior hands of apes and the feet of man are apparent only, that they were based on *physiological* and not on *morphological* considerations. The apes are just as good bimana as men are, and men are just as good quadrumana as the apes. In neither are the posterior limbs in all respects homologous to the anterior. The tarsal bones are differently arranged from the carpal bones, and there are three distinct muscles serving to move the foot that are wholly wanting in the hand. But all this is as true of the apes as of man. The limited opposability of the great toe in man is only a functional distinction. The muscles of opposability are all present; they are merely atrophied by disuse and adaptation to altered conditions. Traces of this power are found in many savages, who hold on with their toes to the branches of trees in the forests where they live, and otherwise employ this posterior thumb in a variety of ways which Europeans cannot imitate. There are, moreover, many instances on record of men acquiring extraordinary dexterity in the use of their toes. Every one in this country has seen the exhi-

bitions of the armless man, who travelled through our towns and
displayed marvellous feats performed with his toes. Again, infants
make far more use of their great toes than adults do. Watch a
new-born babe as it lies in its cradle and amuses itself with exercise of its muscular activities; compare the movements of its
hands with those of its feet, and you cannot but be struck with the
comparative indifference with which it manages both. The human
foot, whose careful study has been said to constitute a sure cure
for atheism, and whose wonderful adaptation to the purpose to
which it is applied has been regarded as an unanswerable argument
for the doctrine of design, can therefore be nothing more than a
natural result of the modification of the posterior hand of the ape,
in simple obedience to the mechanical law of adaptation to changed
conditions, while in it are found all the visible elements of that
ancestral organ which the equally monistic law of heredity has
transmitted from our simian progenitors. Huxley, therefore, re-
stores the Linnæan order *Primates*, removing only the *Chiroptera*.
Haeckel, however, would adhere to his order Prosimiae, the lemurs,
for the reasons above stated.

The true apes are primarily divided into two great groups, which
are as distinct geographically as they are anatomically. These are
the *Catarrhinae* or Old World apes, and the *Platyrrhinae*, or New
World monkeys. They differ chiefly in two important respects.
The *Platyrrhinae* have a flat and broad nose, like other animals.
The nostrils open *outwardly*, and are separated by a broad interval.
They have, also, thirty-six teeth, eighteen in each jaw. In both
these respects they *differ* from man. The *Catarrhinae*, on the
other hand, have a somewhat projecting, laterally compressed, and
often arched or aquiline nose, with the nostrils close together and
opening *downwards*. They have only thirty-two teeth, or sixteen
in each jaw. In both these respects they *agree* with man. The
clear-cut, much projecting, and elegantly formed nose of the Nose-
ape (*Semnopithecus nasicus*) would adorn the face of any European
nobleman, while the countenance, taken in its *ensemble*, of *Cercopithecus petaurista* would be sure to call to any one's mind some
not very bad-looking person of his own acquaintance. And yet
these handsome apes are endowed with long tails. Not only is
the number of the teeth of the *Catarrhinae* the same as in man,
but they are distributed in precisely the same manner, namely:—

four incisors, two canine or eye-teeth, and ten molars or grinders, in each jaw.

The *Catarrhinae* are further divided into two groups of tail-bearing and tailless apes. The tail-bearing apes have most probably been developed directly from the lemurs, and therefore constitute the *nineteenth* stage in the descent of man. Our ancient forefathers in this group were perhaps similar to the now living *Semnopithecus*, from which the tailless apes, forming the *twentieth* stage, were differentiated chiefly by the loss of their tail.. These latter bear the greatest resemblance to man, and are called anthropoid apes, constituting the family *Anthropoides*. The family consists, as far as known, of but four genera, *Hylobates*, the Gibbon of southern Asia; *Satyrus*, the Orang of Borneo and the Sunda Islands; *Engeco*, the Chimpanzee of southern and western Africa, and the Gorilla, first discovered by the missionary Wilson, in 1847, on the Gaboon River, western Africa, and afterwards by Du Chaillu. The Gorilla is the largest of known apes, and exceeds the human stature.

To none of these four anthropoid apes, however, can we point as being in all respects the nearest to man. The Gibbon resembles man most in the form of the thorax, the Orang in the development of the brain, the Chimpanzee in the formation of the skull, and the Gorilla in the differentiation of hand and foot, and also in the relative length of the arms. It is therefore evident that man cannot have descended directly from any known living ape. His real progenitor must, in a greater or less degree, have combined all these characters, and has no doubt been long extinct. It is from paleontology that we alone hope for aid in the discovery of this "missing link." The fossil remains of this extinct genus (*Pithecanthropus*) may be looked for with some confidence in the still little known .region of south-eastern Asia, the Malay Archipelago, and throughout central and western Africa.

The comparative anatomy and osteology of these four genera of anthropoid apes have been exhaustively studied by Carl Vogt, Huxley, and others. The final conclusion to which Huxley comes, and which he expresses in the most unqualified and emphatic manner, is that no matter what system of organs we take, a comparison of the modifications in the Catarrhine series leads to one and the same result : that the anatomical differences that distinguish man from the Orang, Gorilla or Chimpanzee, are not as great as those which distinguish these latter from the lower *Catarrhinae* (*Cynocephalus*, Makako, *Cercopithecus*). Therefore, as Haeckel remarks, it is incorrect to say that man has descended from the apes; *he is himself an ape*, and belongs as strictly to the Catarrhine group as the Gorilla or the Orang-outang! He therefore establishes another family within that group, together with the *Anthropoides*, which he calls the *Erecti* or *Anthropi.* This family he divides into two genera, the first embracing the now extinct ancestor of the human race, the *Pithecanthropus* or ape-man, which therefore forms the *twenty-first* genealogical stage, and the second being the genus Homo, or man as we find him, forming the *twenty-second* and last stage in his development from the moner.

Three anatomical distinctions of any importance are all that exist to separate the two families *Anthropoides* and *Anthropi.* One is the more erect posture of the latter—a difference of degree, however, which varies both with the apes and with men. The second is the higher brain development of the latter, which is also only a quantitative distinction. The third and only distinction which can be called qualitative, is the differentiation in the Anthropi of the larynx into an organ of speech. And not even this much can now be fairly said, since it is found that the larynx of monkeys exhibits a much higher state of development than that of other animals.[10] Haeckel, however, regards *Pithecanthropus* as a speechless man, having the erect posture and differentiated brain, but who had not yet acquired the power of articulate language, or the necessary organs for its utterance. For this reason he offers also a synonym for his name *Pithecanthropus*, the equally appropriate one, *Alalus*, the speechless. This, however, is only theory. In point of fact, the erect posture, size and quality of brain, formation of vocal cords, and the origin of articulate speech, must have all advanced *pari passu*, mutually promoting one another, and developing by insensible degrees, according to the universal method of all nature.

To the various races of men as recognized by ethnologists, Haeckel, in harmony with his general system, gives the rank of *species* of the genus Homo. All definitions of the term species having failed to unite upon any absolutely constant character as a condition to its application, the use of it here is justifiable, notwithstanding the ease with which the human races hybridize, and no matter what theory may be preferred of their origin or relationships. Of these species he makes out twelve, and advances an interesting theory of their origin and geographical distribution over the globe; but upon this new field we can here follow him no farther.

In casting a retrospective glance over the vast subject thus hastily passed in review, there are a few salient points which will have most probably, in an especial manner, struck the mind of the reader.

One of these is likely to be the great brevity of the anthropogenetic line,—considering the variety and multiplicity of living forms found on the globe. We perceive that of the seven subkingdoms of animals now recognized, only three are touched by it, viz:—the Protozoa, Worms, and Vertebrates. The zoöphytes, echinoderms, anthropods, and mollusks all branch off either below or at the worm stage, and the transition from the *Tunicata*, a worm-form, is direct to the vertebrata. This, when adequately appreciated, is an astonishing fact, and one which would never have been conjectured but for positive anatomical evidences. Those who believed in a law of development were looking vainly for proof of the derivation of the different types one out of another, and discussing which should be considered lowest, the articulates or the mollusks. They expected to find proof of a series with the radiates at the bottom and the vertebrates at the top. The truth, as it has at last dawned upon us, dispenses with all such speculations.

Equally surprising is the shortness and directness of the transition from the lowest to the highest vertebrates, from the Amphioxus to the Ape. All the vague surmises of some extensive course of descent and lineal relationship among the numerous classes and orders of vertebrates are now also brought to an end. The higher fishes and higher amphibians, the reptiles and the birds, are all left to pursue special routes of their own; and a brief series of easy and rapid transitions through the lowest fish-form, the *Selachia*, and the lowest amphibian-forms, the *Sozobranchia* and *Sozura*, brings us at once to the lowest mammalian stage.

But perhaps the most surprising part of this whole course is its one great stride through the entire mammalian class, from the marsupial to the lemur. All vain expectations of finding some thread of relationship that should lead through the labyrinth of varied mammalian orders, and connect us with the horse, the dog, the elephant, etc., are thus happily set at rest, and we are permitted only to claim such consanguineal relationship with the opossum, the lemur and the ape.

In fact, instead of a long concatenated "*chaine animale*," as Lamarck supposes, the animal kingdom presents rather a tree, spreading from very near the base with almost a whorl of unequal branches or subordinate trunks, each of which is again variously branched, giving the whole the form of an inverted cone or pyramid. At the upper extremity of each of these branches, which have come a long way independently of each other, is found one of the great groups or types of now living creatures, man occupying the highest summit of the vertebrate branch.

Contemplating now the great number of branches that arise at different points, some of which are short and apparently stunted, while others push upward with different degrees of vigor, only one or two reaching truly lofty and commanding positions, the thought forcibly strikes us that this picture reveals the universal tendency of Nature to develop organic forms. We realize that this vital force or *nisus* is constantly pressing at every point, but that as the conditions of life are limited, success is possible only at a few points; that in consequence of obstacles of many kinds, not the least of which are offered by organic conditions themselves that have pre-occupied the field, the degree of success at these points varies widely, and produces all grades of vigor, size, length, and ramification among the branches. The highest and most thrifty branches mark the line of absolutely least resistance; the shorter and less vigorous ones indicate lines offering varied degrees of resistance; while the stunted, dwarfed, and retrograde branches show lines of resistance so great that the vital force barely overcomes it. Finally, all points from which no buds or branches arise teach us over how large a proportion of nature the resisting agencies wholly overbalance the organic tendencies, and no life can originate.

Another thought to which the attentive contemplation of this theme gives rise, is the greater antecedent probability of like organs, occurring in different animals, being *homologous*, than of their being *analogous*. The conditions in which life finds itself placed are so infinitely variable, that the chances are almost infinity to one against the development of the same organ independently at two different times and places. Where the same organ is unexpectedly found in two animals which had not been supposed to be at all related, it affords the strongest evidence that they are either immediately connected by blood, or at least that they have both descended from a common ancestor that possessed that organ. Hence the irresistible force of the testimony afforded by the so-called "rudimentary organs," which none but those who realize this important law can properly appreciate. That analogues do sometimes occur, in obedience to the law of adaptation, cannot, however, be denied; but they usually betray their origin by being formed on an essentially different principle, though in such a manner as to accomplish the same purpose. The wings of birds, bats, and insects are such cases of analogy, in each of which the morphological differentiation is wholly different, while the physiological function is the same. The beak of the Ornithorhynchus is perhaps as near an approach as we have to a true morphological analogue, the descent of that animal from the birds being overruled by a preponderance of evidence against it.

It is this principle, too, which conclusively negatives the presumption which some have advanced, that the aborigines of America may have descended from the New World monkeys. Catarrhine man could never have sprung from a Platyrrhine ape.

It is, moreover, this same biological law which justifies Haeckel in the assumption of so many hypothetical and long-extinct ancestral forms, although no warrant for them is afforded by paleontology. The Gastraea, the Chordonium, the Protamnion, the Promammalia, and the Pithecanthropus are all creatures, not of his imagination, but of stern logic, based on a profound familiarity with all the facts and principles that bear upon the problem. The common origin and blood relationship of all creatures that possess a spinal column, of all that are endowed with five-toed feet, of all that develop an amnion, of all that have the double occipital condyle, of all that suckle their young, of all having the fore and hind feet differentiated into hands, of all that have the catarrhine nose and identical dentition—these are propositions whose demonstration, by the aid of the law of heredity, is as complete and absolute as that of any proposition in Euclid. There is no other way to account for these facts. The chances of these organs being so many independent morphological analogues, produced by adaptation to identical conditions, are but as one to infinity.

Either the dualistic conception of teleological design, i. e., miracle, must be admitted, or else there is no alternative from this explanation.